Developing Dialogue in Northern Ireland

The Mayhew Talks, 1992

David Bloomfield
Lecturer
Department of Peace Studies
University of Bradford

palgrave

First published 2001 by
PALGRAVE
Houndmills, Basingstoke, Hampshire RG21 6XS and
175 Fifth Avenue, New York, N. Y. 10010
Companies and representatives throughout the world

PALGRAVE is the new global academic imprint of
St. Martin's Press LLC Scholarly and Reference Division and
Palgrave Publishers Ltd (formerly Macmillan Press Ltd).

ISBN 0–333–92012–0

This book is printed on paper suitable for recycling and made from fully managed and sustained forest sources.

A catalogue record for this book is available from the British Library.

Library of Congress Cataloging-in-Publication Data
Bloomfield, David, 1954–
    Developing dialogue in Northern Ireland : the Mayhew talks, 1992 / David Bloomfield.
        p. cm.
    Includes bibliographical references and index.
    ISBN 0–333–92012–0
        1. Northern Ireland—Politics and government—1969–1994.
    2. Great Britain—Foreign relations—Ireland. 3. Ireland—Foreign relations—Great Britain. 4. Irish question. I. Title.
    DA990.U46 B555 2001
    941.60824—dc21
                                                    00–053098

10 9   8   7   6   5   4   3   2   1
10 09 08 07 06 05 04 03 02 01

Printed and bound in Great Britain by
Antony Rowe Ltd, Chippenham, Wiltshire

Developing Dialogue in Northern Ireland

Also by David Bloomfield

PEACEMAKING STRATEGIES IN NORTHERN IRELAND

POLITICAL DIALOGUE IN NORTHERN IRELAND

In Memoriam
David Bloomfield Snr
1912–1999

Contents

Preface

The research for this book was funded by a solicited grant from the United States Institute of Peace, and carried out under the auspices of the Centre for the Study of Conflict at the University of Ulster, Northern Ireland. I am greatly indebted to David Smock, Tim Sisk, April Hall and Deepa Ollapally at USIP, and to Seamus Dunn and staff at the CSC. Any opinions, conclusions or errors in the text are all mine, and should not be associated with either institution.

I owe huge thanks to those participants in the Mayhew talks who assisted me either through interview or by making available documents from the talks process. Primary among them are Sir Ninian Stephen and George Thompson, who offered immense help and wonderful hospitality: without their assistance in particular, the result would be a far poorer affair. Other interviewees will become apparent through the text, while yet others prefer to remain anonymous. All of them, in Britain, Ireland, Northern Ireland and Australia, deserve my deepest gratitude. I have tried hard to represent everyone's words accurately; any errors involved are mine alone.

All quotations in the text are referenced, except for extracts from interviews or from talks documents. With unreferenced quotations, their textual context should make their provenance clear.

Regarding terminology, I use the capitalized form of 'Unionist' when referring to Unionist political parties; uncapitalized, the word refers to the broader unionist-voting community.

Finally, my thanks as ever to Kate McGuinness for the world's broadest definition of editorial support.

Dramatis Personae

The following are not complete delegation lists, but simply the names of those mentioned in the text.

Northern Ireland

Alliance Party of Northern Ireland

John Alderdice (leader), Seamus Close, Eileen Bell, Addie Morrow, Steve McBride, Sean Neeson

Democratic Unionist Party (DUP)

Ian Paisley (leader), Peter Robinson, Sammy Wilson, Denny Vitty, William McCrea, Nigel Dodds, Rhonda Paisley, Simpson Gibson, James McClure

Social Democratic and Labour Party (SDLP)

John Hume (leader), Seamus Mallon, Eddie McGrady, Joe Hendron, Sean Farren, Mark Durkan, Dennis Haughey, Brid Rogers.

Ulster Unionist Party (UUP)

Jim Molyneaux (leader), Reg Empey, Ken Maginnis, Chris McGimpsey, Josias Cunningham, David Trimble, Jack Allen, Jim Nicholson, Jeffrey Donaldson.

Republic of Ireland

David Andrews, Minister for Foreign Affairs
Padraig Flynn, Minister of Justice
John Wilson, Tanaiste and Minister for Defence
Dessie O'Malley, Minister for Industry and Commerce

United Kingdom

Sir Patrick Mayhew, Secretary of State for Northern Ireland
Jeremy Hanley, Minister of State for Political Development
John Chilcott, Permanent Under-Secretary
David Fell, head of Northern Ireland Civil Service

Independent Strand Two Chair

Sir Ninian Stephen, Australia, Chair
George Thompson, Australia, Assistant

Introduction
'What We've Done Before We Can Do Again'

Mr Speaker,

I am pleased to be able to inform the House that, following extensive discussions, a basis for formal political talks now exists ...

The British and Irish governments have made clear that they would be prepared to consider a new and more broadly-based [Anglo-Irish] agreement arrived at through direct discussion and negotiation between all of the parties concerned.

The two governments have agreed not to hold a meeting of the Anglo-Irish Conference between two pre-specified dates. All of the parties concerned will make use of this interval for intensive discussions ...

It is accepted that discussions must focus on three main relationships: within Northern Ireland; among the people of the island of Ireland; and between the two governments. Hope of achieving a new and more broadly-based agreement rests on finding a way to give adequate expression to the totality of relationships.

Talks will accordingly take place in three strands corresponding respectively to the three relationships ...

It is accepted by all that it will be necessary to have launched all three sets of discussions within weeks of each other. A first step will be the opening, as soon as possible, of substantive [Strand 1] talks between the parties in Northern Ireland under my chairmanship ...

It has been agreed by all the participants that before long, when, after consultation, I judge that an appropriate point has been reached, I will propose formally that the other two strands should be launched. My judgement as to timing will be governed by the fact that all

*involved have agreed that the three sets of discussions will be under
way within weeks of each other.*

*It will be open to each of the parties to raise any aspect of these rela-
tionships including constitutional issues, or any other matter which it
considers relevant ...*

*It is accepted by all the parties that nothing will be finally agreed in
any strand until everything is agreed in the talks as a whole.*

*Peter Brooke, statement to the House of Commons,
26 March 1991 (abridged).*

It took Peter Brooke, the British Secretary of State for Northern
Ireland, almost 18 months of dogged deal-making to reach the talks
formula which he finally announced to the British parliament in
March 1991. Each sentence of the statement represented weeks or
months of bargaining. Arguments at the time had focused particularly on the Unionist demand for a suspension of the Anglo-Irish
Agreement – eventually resolved by a suspension of the British–Irish
ministerial conferences which were part of the Agreement's workings; and on the timing of Dublin's entry into the talks process –
eventually left largely to Brooke's discretion within certain time-
limits. The three-stranded talks structure to which he alluded in the
statement consisted of:

- Strand 1: the negotiation of a new power-sharing structure for
  the devolved government of Northern Ireland within the UK,
  between the four main Northern political parties facilitated by
  Brooke
- Strand 2: the negotiation of new North–South cooperative structures, between the four Northern parties and the two
  governments
- Strand 3: the negotiation of a new Irish-British treaty to replace
  the 1985 Anglo-Irish Agreement, between the two governments
  with Northern parties represented by observers.

It was assumed that the strands would proceed in numerical
order, each opening within a few weeks of the last. Since different
parties saw the relative importance of the strands differently, the
key banking principle – 'nothing is agreed until everything is
agreed' – meant that any partial successes in earlier strands would

not be implemented until full agreement had been reached in all three.

A pre-specified ten-week negotiating period was agreed between meetings of the Anglo-Irish Ministerial Conference from April to early July that same year. Brooke presided over a fractious and inconclusive round of Strand 1 talks that produced only a few days of actual face-to-face negotiating. (For a full account of the Brooke talks, see Bloomfield, 1998.) Present at the 1991 talks were: the Ulster Unionist Party (UUP), led by Jim Molyneaux; the Alliance Party of Northern Ireland, under the leadership of John Alderdice; the Social Democratic and Labour Party (SDLP), led by John Hume; and Ian Paisley's Democratic Unionist Party (DUP). Sinn Fein and the loyalist political parties were excluded by common consent until such time as they might renounce the use of political violence.

The Strand 1 talks foundered mainly in a morass of procedural arguments over the arrangements for Strand 2. In particular, Unionist negotiators built barriers to dialogue out of arguments over both who would chair the Strand and where the talks would be held. While these were dismissed by many at the time as procedural wrangles, they nevertheless became substantive issues which had to be addressed before negotiations could begin. The initial plan had been for Brooke and the Irish Foreign Affairs Minister to co-chair Strand 2 talks. When Unionists refused to discuss the future of Northern Ireland with a minister of a 'foreign' country in the chair, agreement was then reached to appoint an independent chair. After much dispute and delay, the former Australian Governor-General, Sir Ninian Stephen, was approved as the independent chair for Strand 2. The issue of a venue for the talks was also hotly contested, and took up yet more of the negotiating period. Finally, a formula was agreed that envisaged talks switching between London, Belfast and Dublin.

But the procedural wrangles had used up so many of the planned ten weeks that Strand 1 only produced nine days of full negotiation, and Strands 2 and 3 never opened. Nonetheless, participants accepted, as hindsight increased, that the Brooke talks had served at least a preparatory purpose in setting the pattern of dialogue, and in establishing several of the key procedures for that dialogue: among them, the three-stranded agenda, the banking principle, and – not least – the habit of actually talking directly to each other, after

17 years of protectionist, confrontational megaphone politics. 'What we've done before,' even the UUP leader Molyneaux admitted, 'we can do again' (quoted in Bloomfield, 1998). And there was a widespread sense among participants, despite the lack of measurable negotiating progress, that these talks would resume at some future date.

But once the summer of 1991 was past, every politician in the UK knew that a general election was due some time within eight months, and the chances of restarting the talks receded as the Northern political parties prepared to entrench themselves in vote-winning positions. Through the autumn and winter, Brooke searched for room for movement, but the political will was in short supply, and he himself decided in late 1991 that pre-election talks were a lost cause. His prime minister, John Major, disagreed, however. As paramilitary violence flared in the early months of 1992, Major called together the four Northern Ireland party leaders and pressed them very hard to re-engage. Rather grudgingly, the delegations eventually assembled at Stormont in March 1992 for a brief official plenary meeting of Strand 1. Major made the formal announcement of the general election (scheduled for 9 April) a few days later, and the talks were officially adjourned until the post-election period.

To Brooke's eye, the March meeting was merely an empty gesture. Indeed, very little of substance happened. But at least Major had got the process restarted, if only symbolically. And that symbolism, as so often in Northern Ireland, proved important. Since the previous July, there had been attempts, particularly from the Unionist parties, to insist on starting afresh by hammering out a whole new basis for talks prior to any further negotiation. The March meeting, however, served to commit them to the continuity of the 1991 formula as before, and also to the implication that they would not have recommenced prior to the election if they were not intent on continuing after the election. Few of the parties were totally happy about this position, but privately most of them accepted that a re-engagement was inevitable. Of course, the continuing exclusion of any parties linked to paramilitary violence – Sinn Fein and the emerging loyalist parties, the Progressive Unionist Party (PUP) and the Ulster Democratic Party (UDP) – was taken as read without discussion.

While these events were clear to public view, two significant other dimensions of the context were continuing well out of sight. Firstly, in 1990 Brooke had largely initiated a confidential communication channel between the British government and Sinn Fein. As it developed in Brooke's time and beyond, it became an increasingly significant dialogue focusing on the question of the terms for an IRA ceasefire. No one else knew that these conversations were going on. Secondly, public discussions between John Hume of the SDLP and Gerry Adams of Sinn Fein had taken place in 1988, but been officially broken off that same year in response to nationalist criticism of Hume for consorting with the enemy. Unofficially, however, the discourse had not only continued but deepened over the subsequent years to focus on the terms for a republican rejection of the armed campaign. Again, few outside the direct participants knew of this communication.

And so, throughout the events which follow in this narrative, these two secret conversations were continuing, despite public denials. From time to time, they cast an occasional shadow over the events chronicled here, even though it was only with hindsight that their effects could be appreciated and quantified.

1
'The Best Job in British Politics': April

The first week of April 1992 was full of heightened political speculation in the UK. With the general election scheduled for 9 April, pundits focused on the two most interesting outcomes: either a new Labour government for the first time since 1979, or a hung Tory parliament dependent on the nine Ulster Unionist MPs to maintain the Conservative arithmetic at Westminster. Would there be a professed pro-nationalist Labour government in Westminster? Would the Unionists wield influence over a minority Conservative government? Among Northern Ireland Unionists, the former was their worst nightmare, the latter their fondest dream.

For the UUP, these issues came into particular focus as they pondered the possibilities of Labour's Neil Kinnock in 10 Downing Street and Kevin MacNamara in Stormont Castle. 'If Mr MacNamara is appointed,' remarked Molyneaux, 'there would be limitations to the degree of co-operation we can give. He makes no secret of the fact that he is a republican.' (*Irish Times* 8 April 1992). On the other hand, in the event of a hung parliament, 'the UUP will decide in the interests of the people of the UK in general and of Northern Ireland in particular whether to end the life of the next parliament prematurely' (ibid.). It was a rare UUP member who did not enjoy the attention and beneficence of a pessimistic and demoralized Conservative party. Even *The* [London] *Times* conceded that, 'an informal arrangement [with the UUP] need not be disreputable for the Tories' (*Irish Times* 2 April 1992). Such flirting might have been music to unionist ears, but caused grave concern among the SDLP and in Dublin.

Nevertheless, predictable friction re-emerged between the Unionist election campaigns. There had been a renewal of the long-standing UUP–DUP pact of solidarity in elections. They had agreed that in those constituencies where a nationalist candidate might win over a split Unionist vote, only one Unionist should stand. However, there was tension over two Unionist heartland constituencies. In North Down, the DUP ran a candidate while the UUP did not, but nonetheless the UUP chose to support formally the independent but UUP-friendly incumbent, James Kilfedder. And in East Belfast, the UUP's John Taylor advocated support for another independent Unionist, Dorothy Dunlop, over the DUP deputy leader Peter Robinson. More general and palpable tensions arose from paramilitary attacks, as the UDA killed a Sinn Fein canvasser in Co. Derry. A few days later, the UDA demanded a return to political talks.

Preparing for his own electoral battles, and with an eye on the Irish-American vote, US presidential candidate Bill Clinton entered the New York Democratic Primary pledging to reverse the ban on Sinn Fein president Gerry Adams's US visa, back the MacBride principles on US investment in Northern Ireland, and appoint a peace envoy for Ireland (*Irish Times* 7 April 1992).

In the UK, as the votes were counted in the early hours of Friday 10 April, it emerged gradually that Major had managed a stunning turnaround in the face of predictions of Tory electoral disaster: the Conservatives held on to power, albeit with a much reduced House of Commons majority of just 21. Neither the dream nor the nightmare came true for Unionists. Equally surprising, Joe Hendron for the SDLP narrowly defeated Gerry Adams, the sitting Sinn Fein MP, in West Belfast. The arithmetic in the overwhelmingly nationalist constituency suggested that Hendron's victory owed much to unionist and loyalist electors switching allegiance to the SDLP in a tactical anti-Sinn Fein vote. Overall in the North, the UUP maintained their nine seats, the DUP their three (including Robinson), Hendron's gain took the SDLP up to four, and reduced Sinn Fein to none, and the independent Unionist Kilfedder held his seat.

As the polls closed in London, a massive IRA bomb outside the Baltic Exchange devastated part of the city's financial district. Three people died in the explosion, and many were injured. Early the following morning, another IRA bomb seriously damaged a motorway flyover at Staples Corner in the city, causing months of road repairs and traffic delays. With exquisite timing, the IRA was pointedly highlighting the effectiveness of its bombing of economic targets in Britain.

Over the post-election weekend, opinions were generally agreed that the vote had endorsed a rapid resumption of negotiations with the formula as before. Adams's defeat was interpreted as a vote against violence and in favour of political engagement. When Major announced his new cabinet two days after the election, there was little surprise that Peter Brooke's name did not appear. He was expected instead to stand for election to the Speaker's chair in the Commons, and his replacement was the former Attorney General, Sir Patrick Mayhew. The appointment received polite endorsement from all concerned except Sinn Fein, but privately Unionists worried that, in contrast to the affable and diplomatic Brooke, Major had appointed 'a hard man for a hard job' (*Irish Times* 13 April 1992). 'Patrician' was the word used almost universally to describe Mayhew, a product of the British establishment and with strong connections to the Anglo-Irish Ascendancy. Mayhew was also tainted in nationalist eyes from his days as Attorney General. He it was who had stoutly rejected widespread allegations of a shoot-to-kill policy by the RUC in the 1980s. Nonetheless, Seamus Mallon of the SDLP wished him 'a fair wind', and noted that Mayhew was 'a very good judge of malt whiskey, and he can't be all bad because of that'. But the DUP's Sammy Wilson conceded only, 'We'll give him a honeymoon period all right, but it'll be a short one' (ibid.). Mayhew himself, unlike most of his predecessors, had had his eye on the Northern Ireland job for some time and actually seemed to want the post. (So often in the past, appointments to the post had been made on the basis of punishment or exile for difficult cabinet members.) On his first day in Belfast, he declared it the 'best job in British politics ... I take up my duties with a high heart and a great sense of good fortune, and with relish for the opportunities that lie ahead' (*Irish Times* 14 April 1992). He made no mention, however, of the confidential communication channel with Sinn Fein, which Brooke had reopened, but the republicans were sent a message to the effect that, 'the line of communication would continue as before, and that Patrick Mayhew was "fully on board"' (Sinn Fein 1993, p. 13). At this stage, of course, no-one knew of the secret dialogue, outside the small number of British and Republican personnel involved in the channel.

When Mayhew announced the make-up of his ministerial team on Tuesday 14 April, the welcome was further muted. Two long-serving and fairly popular ministers, Richard Needham and Brian Mawhinney, were removed. Only the most junior member of the previous team, Jeremy Hanley, was retained and given the Political Development brief (which included managing negotiations). The newcomers reinforced the hard-man image. In particular, Michael Mates, who was given the Security brief, was seen as a hard-line, military thinker. The rumour spread through Westminster that Mayhew had summoned Mates to offer him the post, remarking, 'Let's go to Belfast and have some fun!' Both the other ministers, Robert Atkins (Economy) and Lord Arran (Agriculture, Health and Social Services) were viewed as conservative, 'law-and-order men' (*Irish Times* 17 April 1992). With political development now in the hands of a junior minister, and security given to the most senior, there were fears in the North that the political track might be made subservient to a more vigorous security policy. It was a view rein-forced when Mayhew declared on a subsequent walkabout in Belfast that his government's 'overriding objective was the defeat of terrorism' (*Irish Times* 15 April 1992). It sounded disconcertingly like a reversion to an earlier, simplistic British point of view, which saw Northern Ireland primarily as an internal security problem requiring a military solution. With relentless enthusiasm for his new post, Mayhew told Belfast shoppers 'I have a very interesting job, and one which enables me to meet an awful lot of nice people' (ibid.).

Before the election just one brief meeting of the Strand 1 plenary and one of the Business Committee had been held. But it gave Mayhew the basis on which to build, since the parties had agreed, at least in theory, to resume post-election. Away from the spotlight, he dived into discussions about restarting the political negotiations, meeting Molyneaux on Wednesday 15 April, and Hume and Alderdice separately the following Friday. He kept in close tele-phone contact with his Irish counterpart, David Andrews, the Minister for Foreign Affairs, throughout the week, as they worked to re-establish the negotiating arrangements. On Monday 20, he paid courtesy calls to Church of Ireland Archbishop Robin Eames and

Roman Catholic Cardinal Cahal Daly, and on Wednesday 22 he completed his round of leaders' meetings as he invited Paisley to Stormont.

Having spoken to the four leaders, Mayhew now drafted a letter inviting them to recommence talks next week. In his letter, he explained some of his plans. Since both technically and in reality, the proposed talks would build directly on, and be based on the ground-rules agreed for, the Brooke talks of the previous year, Mayhew took the end of those talks as his starting point. In the latter stages of his talks, Brooke's team had tabled a paper entitled 'Realities and Common Themes' in an attempt to summarize the points of convergence and of disagreement between the delegations at that time. Mayhew suggested that the first plenary discuss a slightly revised version of this paper, which he included with the letter. Once that was completed, he had in reserve another discussion paper, 'Options for New Political Institutions', which he wanted to table. In general, as favoured at the March meeting by all delegations, he was open to a process which would devolve more discussion away from the plenary to smaller committees or working groups.

That evening, he announced that a Strand 1 plenary would take place the following Wednesday to reconvene the talks process according to the pre-election formula agreed in March by all concerned. By the weekend, Northern politicians were generally content with the prospect of taking up substantive negotiations where they had left off the previous July; significantly, most Unionists seemed equally resigned to an early opening of Strand 2.

Mayhew and Andrews met officially for the first time at the Anglo-Irish Conference meeting in London on Monday 27 April. Also attending were Padraig Flynn, the Irish Minister of Justice, and Michael Mates, Mayhew's security minister. After the meeting, they announced the official resumption of talks on Wednesday morning at Stormont, 'on the basis announced by the former Secretary of State in the House of Commons on 26 March 1991' (*Irish Times* 28 April 1992). A three-month gap in Conference meetings was announced. Although no specific date was given for the next Conference meeting, it was declared that there would be no such meeting 'before the week beginning 27 July 1992' (ibid.). So there were at least 12 weeks set aside for negotiations.

2
Strand 1:
'Musical Chairs' April–May

On Wednesday morning, 29 April, Sir Patrick Mayhew met briefly with the four party leaders, and then chaired the first Strand 1 plenary meeting. At the suggestion of the two Unionist parties, it was agreed to send Mayhew's paper 'Realities and Common Themes' to a business committee for further revision, so that it could be discussed at the next plenary. Then each party made an opening statement, outlining their view of the 'problem' and summarizing their post-Brooke positions. A press embargo was agreed, and the parties also nominated two members each to the Strand 1 business committee with a brief to organize the agenda and the procedural arrangements for the talks. The party leaders were tight-lipped at the brief photocall which followed.

In the afternoon, the business committee met, with Jeremy Hanley in the chair. The delegations were: Seamus Close and Addie Morrow (Alliance); Peter Robinson and Denny Vitty (DUP); Mark Durkan and Sean Farren (SDLP); and Josias Cunningham and Reg Empey (UUP). As they examined the 'Realities and Common Themes' paper, Robinson complained, with some support, that it had missed its brief: rather than offering a summary of all points of view, it in effect laid out British government thinking. Hanley accepted the criticism, and promised to revise the paper after hearing the committee's comments. As they talked, they agreed to split the paper into two during the revision: one part would reflect the British view of the political realities as they emerged in the Brooke talks, and the other would review the common themes that had emerged in those talks. They scheduled another business committee meeting for the following Monday (the day before the next plenary), when they could discuss these redrafted versions in the morning, before discussing the second paper in Mayhew's armoury, 'Options for New Political Institutions', in the afternoon. And then they began work on the revision. There were some semantic arguments on the paper's language, and some discussion of how completely they could separate out a clear Strand 1 agenda from the other overlapping Strands without overly restricting the discussions. Of course, Unionists preferred to delimit Strand 1 matters strictly, while the SDLP wanted a more flexible agenda since, they argued, the Strands were too closely interlocking to be totally separate. All in all, it was a solid, working meeting mostly free of the rhetoric that had so dogged the plenary-driven Brooke talks. And that was progress enough for one day.

Mark Brennock of the *Irish Times* caught the mood of cautious expectation when he wrote: 'There is some optimism now that, if the talks do founder, this time it will be [on] issues of substance rather than matters of procedural detail.' (*Irish Times* 30 April 1992). But beyond predictably upbeat statements from Mayhew on the way in to the plenary session, very little public comment escaped the embargo.

On Monday 4 May the business committee resumed its discussions. Hanley circulated a redrafted 'Common Themes' paper, and delegates agreed several further changes. In its final form, it was a much shortened and sharpened document, and while it contained one or two points of agreement which had been reached in the 1991 talks – such as the acceptance by all of Northern Ireland's *de facto* status as part of the UK and of the principle of consent in making any change to that – it was for the most part a succinct list of the issues which everyone agreed needed addressing to build a Strand 1 solution, even though they still disagreed on the resolution of those issues. The list included: the need to recognize two identities; the need for local political institutions; the importance of relationships with the UK, Irish Republic and the EC; the need to address 'terrorism' by constitutional means; the desire to have Northern Irish input into security policy; the protection of individual and community rights; and processes for endorsing any agreed settlement.

Hanley noted the recommended changes, and during lunch the

final version was drafted. The committee approved it in the afternoon session, and agreed to present it and the other half of the original British paper, *Realities*, to Tuesday's plenary. The afternoon's business was then to arrange a plenary agenda for the rest of the week. Tuesday's plenary would accept and discuss these two papers, and then begin discussion of part one of Mayhew's *Options* paper (a review of the overall principles which could guide institutional design). Part two, options for specific institutional design, was scheduled for Thursday's plenary. The committee agreed to reconvene following Thursday's plenary session.

At Tuesday's plenary, *Common Themes* and *Realities* were accepted with little discussion, and delegates moved on to examine *Options* part 1 (the overall principles). The UUP gave their opinion of the document orally, while the other parties circulated written responses. In particular, the SDLP tabled a brief paper entitled *Agreeing the Nature of the Problem*, which they had prepared in advance of the new round of talks. In essence, it argued that to agree on a solution required a prior agreement on the problem. It defined the problem as a conflict between two identities, 'or, more precisely, the failure to devise political structures which accommodate the differences between, and allow full and mutual expression to, those two identities.' Rather than try to find a solution by subsuming one under the other, then, of essence was the need to accommodate *both* through 'parity of esteem', a principle central to SDLP policy. The paper argued for the importance of this overarching principle in guiding subsequent discussions.

There was little dissension over *Options* part 1, and the debate on principles ended in the morning session, ahead of schedule. This allowed the business committee to convene briefly to instruct the British team to draw the morning's discussion together into a paper outlining *Common Principles* in time for the afternoon plenary.

The plenary reconvened to read a draft of *Common Principles*. It laid out nine agreed principles which should underpin any new institutional structure for Northern Ireland, and eight further suggested principles. For an hour and 40 minutes, they discussed the document paragraph by paragraph, Paisley himself raising many issues, and looking to Hume and Alderdice for responses. But at this generalized level, there was little serious dissension. By session end, they had refined the wording of a few paragraphs and agreed that a final draft should contain 16 fully agreed – as opposed to any suggested – principles. The day's business was over, and on Thursday they would proceed to *Options* part 2.

It is worth laying out these agreed principles in detail, since they gradually came to develop a broader relevance than the original remit, and continued to resonate at various subsequent points in the talks process. Once agreed, they functioned throughout the talks as a set of benchmarks against which to measure a variety of proposed structures in a variety of contexts. In brief, the principles required that any new political structures in Northern Ireland must be:

a. Based on democratic principles
b. Widely acceptable to both communities
c. Stable and durable
d. Capable of development
e. Workable
f. Encouraging to both traditions
g. Politically inclusive
h. Effective and efficient
i. Innovative
j. Established within a defined UK relationship
k. Competent to manage any relationship developed in Strand 2
l. Capable of developing a direct relationship with the EC
m. Capable of developing relationships with any future devolved institutions within the UK
n. Capable of securing public endorsement
o. Consistent with the maximum possible delegation of authority from Westminster
p. Open to parliamentary scrutiny and public accountability.

On Mayhew's suggestion, Thursday morning's plenary 'banked' the redrafted *Common Principles* paper, and asked for brief, broad-brush presentations from each party on *Options* part 2. The parties' own specific proposals for institutional structures would then form the agenda for the next week. During the presentations, it became clear that the SDLP was remaining at a very general level – until specific proposals were tabled next Monday – while the other three gave insights into their own preferred and proposed institutional structures. It was a close reversion to the positions at the end of Brooke's talks. Those negotiations had broken down for a variety of reasons, but one factor was that the SDLP was refusing to offer specific devolution proposals and insisting on first agreeing broad principles, while the Unionists were rejecting that approach and demanding negotiation over the nuts and bolts of devolution structures. It had generated the distraction of widespread discussion at the time over whether in fact there existed two culturally different approaches to negotiation, generally deductive and inductive in nature, within Northern Ireland's two communities. Such a red herring had served simply to mask the fact that the SDLP had been unwilling to embark upon specific Strand 1 concessions when they could see that there was no chance of opening Strand 2, where they might hope for counterbalancing gains. It was not an area that any of the participants wanted to revisit.

The presentations were over in an hour, and Mayhew called for a short leaders' meeting before lunch. The party leaders met with him for 40 minutes. Tension had arisen between Mayhew's desire to get down to the specifics of political structures, and the parties' wish to discuss first the SDLP paper on identity, to which the other parties had all prepared responses. It was finally agreed that the parties' wish should be facilitated by suspending plenary meetings for the rest of the day, and establishing a special Sub-Committee to discuss the papers on identity. However, it was also agreed that each party should submit their specific devolution proposals on paper before Monday morning's plenary where they could establish another Sub-Committee to discuss the papers in detail. This way, it was hoped, the principles-versus-specifics distractions of the Brooke talks could be avoided, since every party would put forward their specific institutional proposals.

The plenary then reconvened briefly just to endorse the leaders' suggestions, and agree a press statement. After lunch, the Sub-Committee to Discuss the Question of Identities met for its one and only session, lasting four hours. The UUP and DUP offered papers defining the unionist identity, differentiating between that and a Protestant identity, and asserting that 'parity of esteem' should by definition prevent a united Ireland, since unity would automatically subsume a unionist (though not necessarily a Protestant) identity into a nationalist one. The Alliance paper stressed the importance and value of diversity and plural identities, and argued that the task ahead was to agree, not an analysis of the problem as the SDLP argued, but the structural ingredients of a pluralist political framework that allowed for such diversity. Overall, the meeting was important in tabling officially the four statements on the matter, but less than central to the negotiating process which, it was expected, would begin to focus on Strand 1 structures on Monday.

Over the weekend, speculation was already rife about the possible opening date of Strand 2. In contrast to the previous year, Unionist comment was at best positive and at worst neutral on the subject.

On Monday 11 May, the morning plenary was a short affair. There was a very brief report from the Identities Sub-Committee. Then the four devolution proposals were officially tabled. Mayhew asked that the parties forgo any oral presentation on their proposals at this stage, and remit the discussion to a Structures Sub-Committee which would meet for two days and report back to the next plenary on Friday. With all in agreement, the plenary adjourned after 12 minutes.

The next day, Tuesday 12 May, the real business of Strand 1 began in earnest. The Structures Sub-Committee met at 10.30am. to scrutinise the four proposals and identify common areas and clarify areas of disagreement. Their task would then be to report their findings and recommendations back to the plenary. With Hanley in the chair, the parties each had three nominees to the committee: Morrow, Close and McBride for Alliance; Haughey, Farren and Durkan for the SDLP; Robinson, Vitty and Wilson for the DUP; and Cunningham, Empey and Donaldson for the UUP.

It was immediately obvious that there was a significant difference between one of the proposals and the other three. There were, however, similarities among them all. All four plans included an Assembly, elected from existing Westminster wards by some form of PR (although the UUP proposal expressed a weak preference for first-past-the-post). The Alliance proposal envisaged an Executive appointed by the Secretary of State according to party strengths in the Assembly, and thereafter confirmed in office regularly by a weighted majority in the Assembly. The two Unionist parties envisaged a more limited committee system, rather than an Executive, with committees corresponding to government departments and their chairs and membership elected by the Assembly according to party strengths. Alliance proposed back-bench scrutiny committees corresponding to Executive portfolios, with membership and chairs chosen according to party strengths. These three all agreed that parties supporting violence should be excluded from committee membership.

But the truly controversial proposal came from the SDLP. Rather than an Executive, or a committee system, their proposal was based on the EC model and suggested a six-person Commission to oversee government in Northern Ireland. (The EC, the European Community, was soon to be renamed the European Union, the EU.) Three of the Commissioners would be elected in Northern Ireland, with the highest poller taking the chair or presidency, and one each would be nominated by London, Dublin and the EC. The Commission would either function as a Cabinet in itself, or appoint Heads of Department or Ministers for each government department. The relationships between the Assembly, the Commission and any Heads of Department was, the SDLP said, for negotiation in the talks process.

A feature of the 1991 talks had been the SDLP's reluctance to present concrete devolution proposals in Strand 1 until progress in Strand 2 had reassured them that there was no longer any risk of them being trapped into a solely internal solution. Indeed, because of this fear, the SDLP had not offered concrete proposals for an internal solution since a 1980 discussion document. This time, they took the plunge, and it was their radically different take on devolution which drew all the attention, both around the talks table and among observers. Their proposal, albeit for internal Northern structures, nonetheless envisaged an 'internal' body with an 'external' element in its make-up, and reflected as strongly as ever the SDLP's refusal to consider internal Northern solutions in isolation. Indeed, the paper accepted that, 'because of their implications for the wider relationships to be considered in Strands 2 and 3, much of the details in regard to these issues must await consideration in those strands'. While it did fulfil requirements for a devolution structure, the proposal also made the structure heavily dependent on Dublin input, thus once again tying Strand 1-related progress to Strand 2 elements. The Commission model originated in Irish circles in Brussels, and had received the earlier support of Dublin, who had nevertheless worried that it was 'too much to be accepted in one step' by Unionists (*Irish Times* 10 July 1992).

They were not wrong. The idea drew instant and overwhelming rejection from Unionists, who were 'shocked to the core' (*Irish Times* 6 July 1992). Given that the SDLP were in the talks to safeguard and enlarge Dublin's involvement in Northern affairs, while Unionists were there to reduce and protect against just such involvement, the instant polarization over the idea was hardly unexpected.

It certainly was a radical departure from any models under previous discussion or consideration. From a Unionist point of view, it not only allowed Irish influence in the North's affairs, it placed an Irish member squarely at the Northern cabinet table. Furthermore, a quick calculation produced the obvious result that Unionists would win two of the three Northern seats on the Commission, and thus form a two-to-four minority amongst the British, Irish, European and SDLP members. And to implement such a set-up would involve alterations to the constitutional arrangements for Northern Ireland – change on a scale far greater than any envisaged by the Unionists, Alliance or indeed the British government. It had long been a part of Unionist bedrock that the talks should encompass no direct negotiation of Northern Ireland's constitutional status within the UK (whatever the opinions of their British, Irish and nationalist counterparts). 'We didn't come up the Lagan on the last bubble,' muttered one Unionist (*Irish Times* 31 July 1992). But Hume and his party must have known what Unionist reaction would be to such a radical departure. The proposal, they claimed in its defence, was for discussion purposes, and none of it was 'set in stone' (*Irish Times* 16 May 1992).

As the Structures Sub-Committee began its discussions, Peter Robinson immediately complained that the SDLP's plan was so far out of touch with the others that clearly the party weren't interested in negotiating. Nonetheless, they agreed that the Committee's primary task was to clarify positions, rather than to negotiate, at this stage. And so they proceeded to examine the four proposals one by one, beginning with Alliance.

Criticism of the Alliance proposal centred on the Executive, which for differing reasons the other parties all saw as failing the durability test. They discussed this until lunchtime, and then the afternoon session was given over to the SDLP proposal. Durkan and his colleagues argued that the Commission model was designed to build consensus decision-making and to be proof against the sort of destabilization that had brought down the 1974 power-sharing Executive. (Unionist workers had gone on general strike, bringing life in Northern Ireland to a virtual halt for three weeks, demanding that their representatives pull out of the deal done at Sunningdale, England, in late 1973. The Sunningdale conference had attempted to develop both a power-sharing Assembly and Executive of unionists and nationalists in Belfast, and a Council of Ireland by which Dublin would exercise influence in Northern matters.) The involvement of Commissioners from outside Northern Ireland would cement the arrangement within an international context, they insisted.

But the proposal took strong criticism from the Unionist parties and Alliance. They saw it as breaking several of the agreed principles from earlier discussions, and accused it of being undemocratic and unworkable, ignoring Unionist identity, contradicting the acceptance of the North's constitutional position within the UK on which the talks were based, unaccountable to the electorate and the Assembly. In particular, argued Morrow of the Alliance, the strength of the plan's rejection around the table was evidence enough that in practical terms it would not be workable. Moreover, he criticized the SDLP for failing to understand the Protestant community in thinking they might accept a government member appointed solely by Dublin. Robinson added that if Unionists were unable to accept the 1974 Sunningdale agreement, which involved power-sharing with the SDLP and a more distant involvement of the Irish government, they were never going to accept a Dublin nominee to government. The UUP accused the plan of trying to undermine the North's status within the UK by introducing Irish and EC elements into its government. They suspected embryonic joint Irish–British authority.

Finally, Robinson declared the proposal absurd, accusing the SDLP of chicanery and a complete failure to produce anything that might be usefully negotiated upon. To anyone who lived or worked in Northern Ireland, he went on, that kind of proposal was an invitation to war. For the UUP, Cunningham agreed that the whole proposal was undemocratic, unworkable, and well beyond the remit of the Strand 1 talks since it involved far too much Strand 2 subject matter. He dismissed the Commission as an unelected and minimally accountable quango. The day ended with little achieved beyond a widening of the rift between the SDLP and the other parties.

And the following day began on an even worse note. Ireland woke on Wednesday morning 13 May to find the SDLP proposal published in its entirety in the *Irish Times*. The leak had, presumably, come from the UUP, and they certainly were blamed by the SDLP when the Structures Sub-Committee reconvened that morning. Durkan demanded a leaders' meeting to discuss the leak, but it was agreed that this could not happen before Friday morning, because of absences due – ironically enough – to EC business. The party leaders, as well as Mayhew, were due in Strasbourg that day and the next to attend the opening of a promotional exhibition on Northern Ireland at the European parliament.

Once the row over the leak had died down, Robinson demanded that yesterday's minutes be revised to include a forthright statement to the effect that he considered the SDLP's panel proposal to fall outside the remit of the Strand 1 talks, according to the March 1991 formula, and to be in contradiction of both the *Common Themes* and *Common Principles* papers previously agreed. Durkan responded that minuting such comments was less than helpful. But they moved on to examination of the UUP proposal. The SDLP declared their disappointment: the UUP proposal was very short on detail (it consisted of just one page), and bereft of any innovation. Unlike the DUP paper, argued Durkan, the UUP offered nothing on the question of accommodating two identities. In particular, the proposal for straight majority voting in the Assembly was an echo of the old Stormont administration and completely impractical. The UUP countered that the SDLP proposal was just as impractical. The morning continued with attacks from the SDLP and Alliance, and defence from the UUP with a little support from the DUP. In the main, the sparring was between the SDLP's Dennis Haughey and Reg Empey of the UUP. Haughey demanded to know where representation of the nationalist community came in the UUP proposal; Empey insisted that electoral representation was sufficient. Haughey responded that there was nothing in that proposal that respected him as an Irish person in his own country. The opening of the UUP paper – a forthright declaration of Northern Ireland's continuing status within the UK – was, Durkan added, an insult to nationalist identity. When Hanley asked the SDLP what safeguards for nationalist rights they would need to see added to the UUP proposal, their response was that to answer the question would be to get involved in negotiation, which was not the point of the Sub-Committee at this stage, but that whatever safeguards they might seek could not be met by the UUP plan in its current form. More and more, Empey and Cunningham fell back upon the defence that this was merely a discussion paper and not a statement of any fixed position.

The argument continued after lunch. Hanley asked again what alterations might render the UUP proposal acceptable to the SDLP. Haughey repeated that no alterations would suffice. Finally, they moved on to the final proposal, that of the DUP. This paper, too, was criticized by the SDLP team for failing to incorporate any inclusive movement towards nationalists. In both Unionist scenarios, they argued, nationalists would be given only minor, symbolic roles without real power. Robinson responded that the SDLP were resembling children who wanted their jelly and ice-cream so much that they wanted it along with the soup and the main course as well. But if the 'jelly' included a Dublin involvement in Strand 1, he warned, they would never achieve it. Much of the discussion then centred on the lack of an Executive in the DUP plan, and the workability of a committee structure in its stead. The SDLP argued that the plan was too small-scale and needed more sophistication; Robinson countered that since the point of the exercise was to produce a framework acceptable to nationalists as well as Unionists, a lowest-common-denominator approach was necessary. Disagreement gradually resolved itself into an argument about the remit of Strand 1 negotiations, and specifically whether or not acknowledgement of an Irish nationalist identity was the business of these talks or of Strand 2. Durkan and Haughey asserted that they could not wait until Strand 2 opened to decide whether the DUP had plans to incorporate nationalist identity in a settlement, and so on the basis of the plan before them they had to conclude that there was no such accommodation. Robinson asked what they would need to see added to the plan. The SDLP replied that partnership was the key, and that the DUP plan would produce a series of government committees all controlled by Unionist majorities which would permit limited nationalist involvement but not on the basis of partnership.

By 5.45pm, they had finished discussion of the four proposals, and Hanley tried to move them on to consider how to report back to the plenary. But the argument was not that easily stopped. What the SDLP demanded as recognition of a nationalist identity by Irish involvement in governing the North, the DUP saw as creeping Irish unity, or at least a gradualist approach towards joint British-Irish sovereignty. Durkan declared that there was little point in debating models to incorporate Irish identity, since the Unionist parties disagreed with the very principle of involving Irish identity. But Hanley brought the argument to a halt. He needed to leave, to travel to Westminster to vote, and he handed the chair to David Fell, with the intention of having the Sub-Committee concentrate for the evening on drafting a report to plenary.

After a break, the Sub-Committee resumed to discuss and amend a draft report for plenary drawn up by the British team. The essence of this was a request for further discussion time. But the report also outlined areas where the parties had reached agreement: a single-chamber Assembly of around 85–100 members elected by PR; an executive authority of an unspecified shape but with specified powers; a system that included legislative as well as administrative powers. Further, it listed those areas where agreement had been reached in principle, but where further consideration of details was required: the new entity's relationship with UK government structures and with the EC; the continuing role of the Secretary of State; the precise structures of the Assembly and Committees; fiscal matters; and grievance and rights-protection procedures. Finally, it summarized the party positions on the key issues. First, all but Alliance rejected the functionality of an Executive dependent on continuing widespread support in the Assembly; the Unionists had thus proposed that such power rest in committees, and the SDLP had suggested a Commission. Secondly, the SDLP alone insisted that the need to incorporate an expression of both identities required that the new structure reflect the wider (i.e., Strands 2 and 3) context. The other parties saw this as producing an undemocratic structure and argued that such incorporation could best be managed in a Strand 2 context. Thirdly, the Unionist parties argued that Committee memberships and chairs, distributed according to party strengths, would give nationalists proportionate influence in the structure, while Alliance and the SDLP saw this as too limited. Finally, all but the SDLP had proposed ways to exclude any groupings condoning violence from a share of power. At a little after 8pm, the delegates finally ended their day.

But that afternoon, arriving in Strasbourg for the exhibition launch, SDLP leader Hume had declared himself 'furious' at the flouting of the agreed press embargo, which had led to the leaking of the entire SDLP proposal. Paisley also expressed his anger (*Irish Times* 14 May 1992). Hume had clear reasons to be angry that his party's first concrete proposal in twelve years on governing the North had been leaked before any substantial discussion of it at the table, and he knew that anti-devolution elements – obviously in Sinn Fein, but also among some SDLP members – could pounce on the paper as a sell-out. Paisley too was annoyed even to be seen to be involved in discussing any such heresy which implied the possibility of tinkering with the constitutional status of the North within the UK. Following the formal exhibition dinner, Mayhew met in private with Hume and Paisley, notably excluding senior UUP members who were at the dinner, to mollify the two men and win from them a commitment to continue with the talks process.

Back at Stormont on Friday morning, Mayhew discussed the leak with each party leader separately, and then with all four together, as scheduled. He won their endorsement of a strong statement for the press: 'We are not going to reward the perpetrator by allowing our consultations to be halted, or interrupted, by this episode ... [Any] agreement ... will only be achieved if the talks proceed in private. All the participants are agreed on this' (*Irish Times* 16 May 1992). The leaders also agreed that the Structures Sub-Committee had done good clarificatory work, but that it was now time for real negotiation and that this should take place in plenary. Meanwhile, the Structures Sub-Committee reconvened, reverting to the previous day's argument, the SDLP finding itself again on the defensive over its Commission proposal.

In the afternoon, the plenary assembled, initially to engage in recriminations over the leak, and then to accept formally the Structures Sub-Committee's progress report, *New Political Institutions in Northern Ireland*. It had been an argumentative week for all involved, and Unionists were still publicly expressing a degree of frustration over the shock of the SDLP's proposal. One Unionist told the media after the day's talks that, despite their objections to the proposal, 'no-one has pulled down the shutters. We will be at the [next] meeting in Stormont on Monday' (ibid.). It was enough at the end of a hard week.

But a more formal Unionist response came on Sunday, when the DUP's Sammy Wilson issued a press release, declaring that if the price of talks was a permanent position for Dublin in the North's government, 'there was no business to be done'. He went on, 'We will not trade Articles 2 and 3 for a Dublin seat in the Executive of Northern Ireland. That would simply be conceding to Dublin's demand for a united Ireland' (*Irish Times* 18 May 1992). The Articles to which he referred were those in the Irish constitution, Articles Two and Three, which made a territorial claim to Northern Ireland. Changing these was understood to be the core concession which the Irish government would have to make as part of any satisfactory overall agreement. But that was a matter for Strand 2, when Dublin would enter the process. Put in very simple terms, the Unionist parties had come to the table primarily to negotiate a Unionist-SDLP power-sharing structure for Strand 1, and to tightly limit Dublin's indirect involvement in Strand 2 cross-border structures; the SDLP proposal required that they share Northern power directly with a Dublin member of the cabinet. 'It is', said the UUP's John Taylor, 'an outrageous proposal' (*Irish Times* 21 May 1992).

On Monday 18 May, full delegations returned to Stormont for plenary discussion of the four devolution proposals. The morning consisted of Hume presenting the SDLP proposal, and then taking criticism on it from all sides. But his performance was less than impressive. He had arrived dishevelled and late for the meeting, and had taken some notes prepared by one of his delegates and read them verbatim. His own delegation were disappointed in his disorganization. The Unionists, and to a lesser extent Alliance, continued to castigate the nationalist party for having proposed the Commission either in an attempt to move the goalposts from their original remit or in order to halt Strand 1 negotiations, knowing that Unionists could never accept the idea. Robinson declared that if the SDLP proposal was put to the electorate, no one in the room would get re-elected. Alderdice wondered aloud how such a plan could ever be sold to the inhabitants of the (predominantly Protestant) Newtownards Road in east Belfast. Robinson replied that anyone trying to do so would be lynched. Hume fared poorly under fire from Robinson and others.

After lunch, a reinvigorated Hume had the opportunity to reply to the criticisms of the morning, and he gave a long defence of the SDLP plan, but by this stage even the British team was expressing some doubts over its viability. The arguments over the Commission ran on all afternoon, and neither side was yielding. As frustration built, the UUP began to accuse the SDLP of purposely holding up both progress in Strand 1 and progress to Strand 2, by forcing them to negotiate over a proposal which could never be agreed to. In response, Hume suggested simply taking the two agreed papers, *Common Themes* and *Common Principles*, as the basis for agreement in Strand 1 and moving on to Strand 2, and the sooner the better. But Molyneaux demanded more detailed progress towards a devolution formula before Strand 1 could be called successful by any measure. Hume suggested that perhaps if both Strands ran concurrently, that might help them to deal with the overlapping question of Irish identity in new structures. But the UUP again refused, saying that since Strand 2 was to discuss the relationship of a Strand 1 entity with Dublin, to do so without a clear sense of the shape of that entity would be negotiating in space. Why couldn't the SDLP accept a more prosaic power-sharing framework for Strand 1 and move on to Strand 2?

Mayhew picked up on the argument, reminding everyone that nothing was agreed until everything was agreed, and suggesting that maybe both the SDLP and the Unionist/Alliance proposals could continue to be fleshed out while Strand 2 got underway. But Unionists countered that they could not possibly move to negotiations with Dublin without the safeguard of a solid devolutionary structure agreed first. They could do no more than agree to meet again tomorrow.

There seemed little common ground emerging between the viewpoints, and in particular between the radical novelties of the SDLP's proposal and the much more conservative Unionist plans for limited administrative power-sharing. The debate continued throughout Tuesday 19 May, as technically the delegations took turns to present their own proposal and answer questions on it. But the discussion continually circled back to the basic split: the SDLP accused the other parties of failing to build in any mechanism to give any real accommodation to the nationalist identity, while the others in turn accused the SDLP of going much too far in demanding a Southern member of a Northern cabinet. In essence, it was an argument about the remits of Strands 1 and 2, and a reflection of the parties' own differing prioritizations of these Strands. For Unionists, Strand 1 could only debate an *internal* structure for the government of Northern Ireland – and thus the SDLP proposal of involving the Irish government was far beyond this remit. For the SDLP, the internal frameworks on offer from the other parties could not be agreed to unless they were strongly balanced by Irish involvement.

On Wednesday, the parties discussed the DUP proposal, the last of the four. But again the same argument resurfaced. Instead of putting detailed questions to Paisley after his presentation, Mallon immediately asked what the DUP thought existed in their proposals that might possibly weld a divided community together. And off they went once again into the argument over Strand 1 versus Strand 2 matters. By the end of the morning, Mayhew adjudged the discussion finished, and adjourned for lunch. Afterwards, they reconvened briefly to agree that Mayhew and the party leaders would meet at Westminster the following day, and that the plenary would resume on Tuesday of the following week to consider how to proceed. They approved a minimal press release of three sentences, and the talks ended. By now, every detail had been discussed in each proposal, but little agreement had been reached. 'I think at this moment we are trying to explore just how flexible each other party is,' commented one Unionist. 'At least we are talking, but I can't say yet if we are getting anywhere' (*Irish Times* 21 May 1992).

The lack of progress was beginning to worry the Dublin government, who were anticipating an early start to Strand 2 talks. Strand 2, it had been agreed, would begin 'within weeks' of Strand 1, at the Secretary of State's discretion in consultation with the Northern parties, but with the hope that Strand 1 progress would have been made by then. None was so far apparent. For six months in 1990–91, Peter Brooke had refereed a bitter battle between Dublin and the UUP about the proposed timing of the Irish government's entry into a talks process. There seemed a danger that this row might now reignite. With no way forward emerging, expectations were that Mayhew might try to take the initiative in formulating the future agenda, to avoid what was beginning to look like the all-too-familiar wrangling over details that had characterized the 1991 talks.

Focusing on the two central priorities, the need for Strand 1 progress and the opening of Strand 2, Mayhew spent Thursday morning in meetings at Westminster with Molyneaux, Hume, Paisley and Addie Morrow of Alliance. But there was no break-through. Then he faced his first Northern Ireland Question Time in the House of Commons as Secretary of State. Most of that discussion centred around the recent behaviour of a British Army regiment in Coalisland, and expressions of Unionist outrage at David Andrews' demand that the regiment be withdrawn. On the topic of the opening of Strand 2, Mayhew remained inscrutable.

Over the next few days, he maintained contact with the party leaders, but there was little progress, and the Strand 2 question continued to raise doubts. The crux of the problem was of course in Strand 1. By this stage, the hope had been that all the proposals would have been tabled, and out of them a compromise structure for devolved government would have arisen. Instead there was impasse. Unionists complained that the SDLP proposal strayed beyond the remit of Strand 1 by bringing in Irish government involvement in the shape of a Commissioner. Such Irish involvement was exclusively the business of Strand 2. The SDLP, in turn, was reluctant to accept any solely internal structure without a parallel Unionist acceptance of Irish involvement. Unless some minimal structure was agreed in Strand 1, Unionists were highly unlikely to agree to participate in opening Strand 2. One of them commented, 'They're all playing musical chairs because they're afraid of being blamed [for the impasse]. They're running around in circles trying to see who'll get caught when the chair is pulled out' (*Irish Times* 26 May 1992).

For his part, over the weekend Molyneaux was once again wondering out loud about the possibilities of a settlement in which Northern Ireland would get the same degree of partial devolution from Westminster as was planned for Scotland and Wales, a proposal as dear to his own heart as it was contradictory of the whole three-stranded process. As ever, the UUP leader's commitment to the overall process was undefined. While making no progress on the Strand 1 agenda, Mayhew did however suggest that the four party leaders should meet soon 'informally' in London with the Strand 2 chair, Australian Sir Ninian Stephen. Stephen and his assistant, the high-ranking Australian civil servant George Thompson, had taken up position in London, ready for the opening of Strand 2. The party leaders consented, as long as the meetings were kept low-key and very unofficial, and it was agreed to present Stephen publicly as simply passing through London on other business. It was an initial attempt to at least focus minds on Strand 2.

On Tuesday 26 May, Mayhew spent most of the morning in meetings with the party leaders. He presented them with a third British paper outlining areas of agreement in Strand 1, but it failed to break the deadlock. Paisley and Molyneaux were adamant that Strand 2 could not open until there was substantial agreement in principle on the shape of an internal settlement which did not include Irish government involvement. Hume was equally firm that Strand 1 could not be completed without discussing the modalities of Dublin's involvement, which meant opening Strand 2.

One brief plenary meeting was held. Paisley declared that the sticking-point was Hume's assertions that majority decision-making was unacceptable in government and that nationalist identity needed to be represented by the Republic's government. Hume in turn blamed the lack of progress on an inability of 'some parties' to consider the question of relations with the rest of Ireland. Alderdice said he saw no grounds for any optimism at this stage.

Mayhew summarized the position: there were two essentially different models emerging, and no sign that either side was prepared to move from its position. The situation was grave. He tabled a new British paper, *Models of Government*, and suggested that they re-establish the Structures Sub-Committee for a limited time to discuss the paper and try to break the deadlock. The parties acceded to the idea, and agreed further to table party papers to the Sub-Committee specifically concerning the impasse and its causes. They also agreed not to officially minute the deliberations of the Sub-Committee, which would meet on Wednesday and Friday, and report back to plenary on Monday. At this stage events were promising little more than a rerun of the Brooke talks, with the same sticking-points over the same issues bringing deadlock.

Breaking down into the smaller committee structure, and forgoing the formalities of official minutes, seemed a last chance to deepen the quality of the dialogue and move it beyond the rhetoric to explore real possibilities for progress.

3
Strand 1: 'An Air of Optimism': June

As agreed at the previous day's plenary, the Sub-Committee duly met all day on Wednesday 27 May, to consider in the first instance the four papers from the parties regarding the ongoing deadlock. The paper tabled on Tuesday by the British, *Models of Government*, was instantly forgotten. Each of the papers tried to define the elements of the impasse. *The Nature of the Blockage*, another one-page note from the UUP, placed the blame squarely on the SDLP, for two reasons. First, they complained that: 'John Hume believes that any govt in NI [*sic*] should not come from or be responsible to the elected assembly.' Second, in terms of involving the Irish Nationalist identity in a new institution, the SDLP were claiming that 'their presence in such an institution, even at the highest level, is insufficient to meet this requirement'. Instead, the presence of the Irish government in a local institution, 'can achieve the objective of obtaining loyalty from Nationalists in NI in a way that the presence of the SDLP cannot'. In UUP eyes, the proposal for externally appointed commissioners 'is contradictory to their support for para 2 of "common themes" [*sic*] document'. The reference was to the first theme among 14 identified and agreed during the negotiations of early May. Entitled 'Constitutional Status and Guarantee', it read in part: 'It is accepted by all the talks participants that Northern Ireland is *de facto* a part of the United Kingdom; that there should be no change in that position without the consent of a majority of the people who live there.' 'The SDLP paper', claimed the UUP, 'is not consistent with the continued membership of NI within the UK.'

The DUP paper, *Impediments to Progress*, explored a similar theme at greater length. '[I]n essence, the impediments are (1) the SDLP demand for the government of the Republic of Ireland to be involved in any internal Northern Ireland institution, and (2) the SDLP refusal to participate in or support any structure for Northern Ireland that operates on the basis of any form of majority rule.' The DUP complained that these obstacles 'have never been aired publicly prior to the commencement of this [talks] process', and voiced the suspicion that they had been dreamt up purposely to derail the negotiations: 'with premeditation, the SDLP sought to widen the gap [and] ensure the failure of the Talks process.' They warned that the unionist community would reject such an unpalatable proposal and, in the process, reject constitutional politics. The idea of an Irish Commissioner, they argued, was far beyond what the SDLP found acceptable in the Council of Ireland proposal of the Sunningdale Agreement of 1973. It was the DUP's belief that incorporating the Nationalist identity in the settlement was more properly the business of Strand 2, and they urged the SDLP to drop the idea and agree a more mundane Strand 1 formula with the safeguard that, if they did not receive satisfaction in Strand 2, then the banking principle would save them from implementing anything against their will in Strand 1. On the question of majority votes in the Assembly, the DUP quoted from the first paragraph of the *Common Principles* paper: 'It is agreed that these institutions should be based on democratic principles and reflect the wishes of the electorate.' Given that even the SDLP's own proposals include some majority-vote decision-making, the DUP 'need the conflicting messages cleared up'.

The Alliance paper, *The Strand One Problem*, had a similar focus. The main impediment was 'SDLP insistence that the Irish Government ... must have a direct involvement in any new decision-making body in Northern Ireland through the appointment of a "commissioner"'. Believing that their own plan for executive power-sharing was sufficient to express the needs and identity of nationalists, for Alliance the Commission proposal 'amounts to a major change in the constitutional status of Northern Ireland within the United Kingdom', and was thus outside the remit of the talks. Alliance was also 'deeply disturbed by the strongly expressed SDLP view that they would be completely opposed to any power being devolved to any elected Northern Ireland body', an approach which would provide 'no effective local democracy at all'. But Alliance had criticisms of the Unionist parties too. Their proposals thus far did not offer a sufficiently 'effective and influential role for non-Unionists. Their reluctance to accept executive power-sharing encourages a suspicion that a majority in the Assembly might be used to deny minorities any real say in decision-making ... They have consistently rejected the Anglo-Irish Agreement but have not yet revealed any alternative proposals.'

The SDLP paper, *Necessary But Not Sufficient*, was a more defensive affair. The other three parties' formulas for proportionality and power-sharing were, in the SDLP view, 'necessary but not sufficient to address ... different identities and different allegiances based on those identities'. While they addressed the important issue of fair representation, they ignored equality of *political identification*, preferring a solution 'explicitly predicated upon an *exclusively* British context'. For the SDLP, Unionist Britishness was no more and no less important than nationalist Irishness, and there must be real *parity of esteem* between the two, rather than merely some degree of acknowledgement of Irishness within a UK context. For this reason, 'the role of the Irish Commissioner is set alongside that of a British Commissioner, to act together as expressions of and guarantors of the two basic identities.'

For all the subtleties of argument presented, it was clear to see that the row was pitching traditional Unionist goals against traditional nationalist goals. Installing a Dublin-sponsored cabinet minister in Belfast was obviously interpretable as a step towards weakening British control of the North. The Unionists were bound to see it as a challenge to the North's constitutional status. On the other hand, the arithmetic of the North dictated that setting up an assembly with a majority-vote system, or an executive with party-proportional membership, was an attempt to return to at best Sunningdale and the 1974 power-sharing Executive, if not to the old majority-dominated Stormont, and thus exclude nationalists from a real share of control. If these were negotiating positions, then work could be done. But if they were bottom lines, the prospects were bleak indeed.

Wednesday was taken up arguing through the two key points of the impasse. The SDLP explained at length the thinking behind the

Commission proposal, and talked up its advantages (high-profile external representation in Brussels, for example), while the Unionist reply was that it was impossible to implement: it was so close to joint authority, and so far in excess of Sunningdale, that it would merely provoke 1974-style loyalist violence. They argued for and against methods of achieving consensus decision-making and weighted majorities in an Assembly.

But there was some progress beyond this black-and-white restatement of positions. Individuals like Reg Empey and Sean Farren were considering the *process* of their discussions, rather than the *content*. For them, one possibility which was opening up was that of finding enough common ground – perhaps an unfinished model of government, or one presenting alternatives for various ingredients – to permit moving ahead to further Strand 1 work (and, logically, to an opening of Strand 2). At one point, Robinson repeated the accusation that the SDLP proposal was outside the remit of Strand 1, as defined in Peter Brooke's March 1991 statement and in 'other documents'. This latter reference was to something that Unionists occasionally claimed to have received from Brooke: a letter or series of letters which responded to requests Molyneaux and Paisley had made for clarification of the statement. It had been a regular suspicion of the SDLP and Alliance that such correspondence existed, and that it offered guarantees from the British government to the Unionists concerning the durability of the Union. The accuracy of that suspicion remains undefined.

The Sub-Committee resumed on Friday morning. The atmosphere at Stormont that morning was already gloomy, with rumours abounding of secret meetings between NIO officials and delegates from the Unionist parties. Amidst such suspicions, the SDLP's Haughey raised the question of the 'other documents' that Robinson had mentioned in Wednesday's session, and a long and somewhat rancorous discussion ensued, with Haughey demanding assurances from Unionists that no other documents or statements had authority over the March 1991 formula, while both Robinson and Empey claimed that the SDLP devolution plan could only have come from a party intent on breaking from the talks. 'The problem', reflected one SDLP delegate later, 'was to convince the Unionists that we were serious.'

David Fell, in the chair that morning, tried to summarize the possibilities for progress. They could either re-engage in the substantive arguments by trying to design a whole new model for the North's government, or they could concentrate on the process of their discussions – agreeing where progress was forthcoming and where it was lacking – and look for ways to bank what they had and to move ahead to further stages of negotiation without complete success in this early one. Fell favoured the second tactic, and offered a two-paragraph paper in which he suggested a 'park-and-ride' approach. They could 'park' the SDLP model for the time being, and open discussions in Strand 2 with the Unionist model assumed as the notional Strand 1 blueprint, returning later, after progress in Strand 2, to hammer out the final shape of the Strand 1 formula. Haughey objected that it involved downgrading the SDLP proposal, and was thus unacceptable. Robinson countered that, since everyone's model would be downgraded, they would share that problem.

Fell offered another option. In a twin-track approach, neither Strand 1 model would be chosen definitively, but both would continue to be worked up, while they moved forward into Strand 2. The SDLP accepted this approach, but no one else agreed. Robinson suggested both the park-and-ride and the twin-track approaches be operated, without any prejudice to any result or any party. But everyone else rejected the idea. Fell continued to push for movement into Strand 2 and also Strand 3, but there was little Unionist enthusiasm for it.

Robinson then suggested two elements for their report to plenary. First, they would continue to prepare a new devolution model, one which they could all broadly support but with some qualifications, but one which, at least for the moment, did not incorporate any means for the expression of nationalist identity beyond political participation in an executive and/or assembly. Second, they would agree on a statement of principle regarding the need to reach agreement over the expression of identity. It appealed to SDLP negotiators, who in turn offered three elements. First, they continue to work on a further refinement of a devolution model, with options for parties to reserve their positions on some of the ingredients. Second, they agree a statement on the principle of including expression of identity in the formula. Third, they agree to progress to Strands 2 and 3, and to revisit subsequently the devolution argument of Strand 1 in the light of progress in the other Strands. Finally, they could therefore report to plenary that they had not reached agreement but had identified a path for progress.

The flaw in this for Robinson, of course, was the progress to other Strands. The DUP position on opening Strand 2 was still very firm: it was dependent on substantive prior progress in Strand 1. The three Strands, Robinson told the Sub-Committee, were sequential and consequential, that is, each followed from the earlier one, and each could only open following progress in the earlier one. (In fact, Robinson was being disingenuous. After long negotiations through 1990–91, Brooke had removed the original requirement for 'substantive progress' in Strand 1 before Strand 2 could open. Only the DUP continued, throughout the Brooke and the Mayhew talks, to insist on it as a precondition.)

Empey, setting aside the question of *when* to open other strands, agreed that there was no reason not to move 'backwards' between Strands. Sufficient doors could be kept open along the way for a return to Strand 1; indeed they could agree a formula which included the specified right to do so.

The SDLP offered to circulate a brief paper which contained a proposal for moving ahead, and asked that it be read over lunch and discussed when they resumed. Over the dining table, the SDLP Sub-Committee representatives met with Fell to discuss his and their papers. They were of the opinion that it was possible to marry the two.

But the afternoon session began with a strong attack on the SDLP paper, which Farren defended. Farren suggested the paper could at least provide some methodology for fleshing out the existing points of agreement. Gradually, the focus of discussions shifted away from the disagreements on the table to the areas of agreement. At 4pm, Hanley apologized that he would need to leave in 15 minutes, and they broke up from the formal setting and left the negotiating room.

Immediately, a spontaneous series of informal bilateral meetings began to happen around the building – 'corridoring,' in the terms of one delegate. Suddenly the speed of exchange had multiplied. Hanley postponed his departure for an hour. A series of short papers began to circulate, possible drafts of a sketch of the report to plenary. Hanley again delayed his exit until 6.30pm. By then, one paper had gone through four rapid amendments to emerge as an acceptable report for plenary which would permit some forward movement in the talks. It had managed some synthesis of view-points.

The paper, *Political Talks: Report of the Sub-Committee Established on 26 May*, identified three issues of dispute:

a. the perception that the SDLP refused to contemplate any form of 'majority rule'
b. the Unionist and Alliance conviction that the Commission plan could not be sold to the unionist community
c. the SDLP's sense that they were being forced to abandon their entire proposal before any progress could be made.

The report also offered clarificatory comments on these issues:

a. The SDLP explained that they were indeed opposed to any simple majority system that would preclude any meaningful role for Nationalist representatives, and argued for a classification of issues into contentious (requiring a negotiable degree of weighted voting) and non-contentious (decidable by simple majority).
b. The SDLP – with general support – reasserted that any outcome should give effective expression to both main traditions, declared that their formula fulfilled this requirement, but confirmed that they were open to considering other means to achieve this.
c. The Unionist parties assured the SDLP that their proposals would be treated exactly as those of any other party.

Finally, the report suggested some means of making progress. It asked for plenary's approval to continue the Sub-Committee work, focusing on *Common Themes, Common Principles,* and the Structures Sub-Committee's progress report, and in particular that report's list of areas needing further work to produce agreement. They suggested that this should be possible if parties held the right to reserve their positions on various specific points. They also stated for the record that the expression of both identities should be an integral part of the overall settlement, and that parties should also reserve the right, in case of progress in the other Strands, to review Strand 1 agreements.

When the delegation reported the day's work to Hume, he was enthusiastic, even beginning to talk about possible compromises on the Commission proposal. That set the tone, as informal discussions continued into the weekend. Such progress was made that by Sunday a series of other draft papers had become attached to the report, each outlining in greater detail specific sections of a possible formula for agreement. Among them was a devolution proposal, based on an overall Unionist–Alliance model of elected power-sharing government, but with an overseeing Panel corresponding closely to the SDLP's Commission.

Monday 1 June was the beginning of the sixth week of talks, and Dublin was getting impatient to get involved in Strand 2. The terms for opening Strand 2 'within weeks of Strand 1' had always been unofficially agreed to mean a maximum delay of five weeks. But the delicacy of Strand 1 arguments at this stage disinclined the Irish government from pushing too hard on the matter, at least in public. They satisfied themselves with making the British aware of their impatience.

No formal session was held on Monday morning, in order to allow time for the delegations to hold internal discussions to bring each other up to speed on the weekend's events, and for a meeting of the four party leaders with Mayhew to discuss the Sub-Committee's report. Paisley was not happy about tabling the report in the scheduled plenary, but was overruled, and the leaders agreed to support the Sub-Committee's request for a two-day extension to continue its work. Approaching the negotiating room for the plenary the SDLP delegates met David Fell, who surprised them with the news that he had changed his mind 'about the report'. From his earlier support for the SDLP position of parking Strand 1 and moving into Strand 2, he seemed to have come to accept that it now asked too much too quickly of the Unionists.

The scheduled plenary eventually took place after midday, and lasted five minutes. Its tone was far more upbeat than any before it. At the leaders' behest, the meeting agreed to allow the Sub-Committee to 'continue its deliberations on the basis of the report produced and the papers attached to it' through the rest of Monday and all of Tuesday, and to report to plenary at 10am on Wednesday.

There were a few minutes of congratulation all round for the useful progress achieved and a mention of the dangers of talking to the media at this point, and the plenary once again gave way to the smaller configuration.

The Sub-Committee duly went into session on Monday afternoon. Hanley, in the chair, reminded them that time was against them in this Strand, but that they at least had a partial agreement on paper. Robinson suggested boldly that they had a whole series of issues to be worked upon and agreed, and that they should therefore set themselves a central negotiating framework and move into smaller groups to hammer out the details. To the shock of many in the room, he announced that they should aim for a complete internal package of institutions for Northern Ireland. The SDLP delegation looked stunned. They had been seeking more cautiously for the maximum common agreement they could manage out of this Sub-Committee process. The mandate from the plenary had modestly instructed the Sub-Committee to 'work towards the greatest possible degree of common ground on new political institutions'. Suddenly the opposition were demanding that all the crunch issues be faced here and now and resolved. Haughey reminded Robinson of the less ambitious mandate they had agreed. Was Robinson ignoring this? Robinson looked irritated. There was a long silence, during which Robinson straightened his tie and sorted his documents while Denny Vitty put on his jacket and rolled up his papers. They looked very much like a delegation on the point of walking out. Hanley called a break to allow Robinson to consult with his delegation.

When they resumed after a long intermission, they divided into two subgroups. Durkan, Robinson, Donaldson and MacBride went off to discuss structures of government. Vitty, Close, Morrow, Haughey, Empey, Allen and Farren focused on the less contentious issues of day-to-day administration. The second group made good progress and had finished by the mid-afternoon tea-break. The first group stayed in session until 9.30pm, gradually moving through the devolution models towards a better synthesis of the power-sharing assembly/executive model and the overseeing Panel.

The whole Sub-Committee reconvened on Tuesday morning. The day was another intense one. At this stage, though, they were well beyond the rhetoric of the earlier weeks, arguing as fiercely as ever but now about the nuts and bolts of the whole devolution structure: defining the powers of the Panel, deciding who would appoint Heads of Departments, the length of service of Committee Chairs, and so on. Through the day this became a much-amended draft, cautiously entitled *Possible Outline Framework (to assist discussion)*. By 11.15pm this document had become a 19-paragraph outline of a structure involving an Assembly, a Panel, a system of Committees/ Departments of government, and a complex set of arrangements to govern the interrelations of power between these elements. There were still issues of disagreement among them, but they were inescapably close to something which, although they all agreed it was cumbersome, appeared to include enough of all four original plans to satisfy most viewpoints. One major sticking point was the Panel. This had been reduced from a Commission, and currently consisted of only three members, all elected from Northern Ireland. The removal of the three external commissioners, in particular the one appointed by Dublin, would represent a major climb-down by the SDLP, and they were not yet in the fold over this point. The Alliance had not got their power-sharing executive in the form they had wanted, either, but they had managed to build stronger power-sharing into the Assembly and the Committees. The Unionists, it seemed, had suffered least. They had managed a compromise version of a committee structure which was not so totally different from their original proposals, and had had to pay by accepting a Panel which was a radically circumscribed version of what they had at first been offered.

Just before lunch the next day, another brief plenary was held to accept the *Possible Outline Framework* document. The plenary agreed that it warranted further discussion, and so decided yet again to extend the life of the Sub-Committee and permit its work to continue in order to report at a plenary in a week's time. Mayhew did remind them all of the urgency of progressing on to Strand 2, expressing his hope that the Sub-Committee's work would lead to success that would enable that move.

And so the discussions continued at their most intense level yet. On that day, Wednesday, they ran on past midnight, and at 12.45am a more substantial draft of the *Possible Outline Framework* was produced. Away from the formal plenary, the Sub-Committee delegates were able to work without any need for official endorsement. So they were able to produce the document, on which they all still held reservations and doubts, on a pragmatic basis, without any official responsibility for endorsing its contents. It was a vital breakthrough. All four Sub-Committee delegations appended initials to the report. On the Unionist side, it was seen as both a breakthrough in progress towards a Strand 1 agreement, and a victory over the opposition. But the euphoria was short-lived. When the SDLP members took the document to Hume he refused to add his initials, and angrily rejected it. 'Hume came down and shouted and yelled and screamed,' claims one UUP delegate. 'He had an enormous row with Mallon, somebody had to physically get between them.'

As time passed, the forward movement slowed. The SDLP had not given up completely on their original Commission model, and they were waiting with some degree of patience for the question of the external Panel members to be discussed. The *Possible Outline Framework* thus far also failed to define explicitly where exactly executive power fell between the Assembly, Executive and Panel. They were a long way from agreement yet. But they continued to work over the following week. As the days passed, however, the remaining differences became more intractable.

By Friday, the SDLP had reintroduced their external commissioners. Attention now centred on more adaptation of the Panel: one option was that all six Panel members could come only from within Northern Ireland; another was that Northern politicians would have a veto on outside nominees. As the seventh week of talks began, they sat again on Monday and Tuesday. By Tuesday evening, they were not yet ready to report, and begged an extra day's grace from the plenary. It was agreed that Thursday 11 would be the deadline day. The Sub-Committee would make its final recommendation to the plenary, and a decision would also be made about Strand 2. Rumours had been circulating that Prime Minister Major might be about to throw his own weight behind the talks process, and he was scheduled to hold a summit meeting with Reynolds on the same day, in the margins of the Earth Summit in Rio. Reynolds was fully expected to demand movement on Strand 2, since its opening was already two weeks behind schedule. (But at the same time it was accepted that the following week was a busy one for the Irish government in general and the Department of

Foreign Affairs in particular, as ratification of the Maastricht Treaty and other weighty matters would preoccupy the Dail.) That only increased the general sense of impending deadline.

The Sub-Committee produced its final report on the evening of Wednesday 10 June. It had, it reported, succeeded in fulfilling its mandate to search for 'the greatest degree of common ground' on a devolution structure, but there was obviously still some significant distance to be crossed between the SDLP and the others. The report included a series of annexes, most importantly the final draft of the *Possible Outline Framework*, and a draft Code of Practice which aimed to specify roles, responsibilities and decision-making powers of Departments, Committees and the Assembly. The *Possible Outline Framework* comprised a series of component parts, among them:

- a single, unicameral Assembly of 85 members elected by PR. With a Speaker elected by a weighted majority of probably 70 per cent, the Assembly would exercise power through a system of Departmental Committees, one for each area of government. Committee Chairs, Deputy Chairs and memberships would be allocated by party strength in the Assembly, possibly by the D'Hondt formula. Committee Chairs might also be Heads of Departments
- a separately elected three-member Panel with significant powers yet to be defined, but likely to include consultative, monitoring, referral, arbitration and representational capacities, the approval of appointments, etc.
- executive and legislative responsibilities for 'transferred' matters (those government areas to be handed over from Britain immediately), and potentially for 'reserved' matters if durability and stability were proved (those areas to be handed over in due course at Britain's discretion)
- legislation would require majority support in the relevant Committee and in the Assembly; contentious issues would require a weighted majority
- a Bill of Rights and other civil rights safeguards.

There were additional papers attached to the report: an all-party draft on the roles and responsibilities of Committees and their Chairs; a brief outline of potential arrangements for Departmental budget allocations; a British paper on ensuring fair roles for all traditions; one paper from each party on possible weighted majorities (the Alliance and UUP preferred 70 per cent; the DUP wanted 65 per cent; and the SDLP 75 per cent); and a draft paper on relations between a new Northern Ireland structure and the EC. (The main provisions of the *Possible Outline Framework* are outlined in Appendix 1.)

Again some excitement started to build around the Stormont corridors and among the press outside. But although the negotiators had moved some of the details on from the previous week's midnight draft, still they had not quite achieved consensus. The Unionists and Alliance were ready to endorse the *Possible Outline Framework*, but the SDLP had moved back from the brink. As the report outlined in its introduction, the SDLP chose to reserve its position on several of the key ingredients: the authority of Heads of Departments and their relationship with Departmental Committees; arrangements for legislation; and Departmental budgetary arrangements. Furthermore, throughout the component parts of the report there were items noted for further discussion, or sections limited to outline status. A lot more work would still need to be done to square the circle of Strand 1. Additionally, the Sub-Committee had seen the circulation of papers on a variety of topics, including human rights safeguards, finance, a Bill of Rights, and so on, which it had not had time to address. So the report was not an agreement, but it was a statement of measurable progress. Something, finally, however tentative, had come out of Strand 1 discussions.

On Thursday morning, the plenary convened. The key issues for discussion were the Sub-Committee's report, and the question of movement to Strand 2. Hume explained that his party had not endorsed the final report for several reasons. They still had doubts about the workability of the whole plan, and still wanted to see a clearer separation of powers between the Assembly and other institutions. And, finally, they felt that the key issue of identities and allegiances had still not been fully addressed. However, he accepted that both Unionist parties had assured him that identities would be addressed in Strand 2. Molyneaux, with Paisley's support, demanded that Mayhew now offer an official British view on the devolution plan. He felt that it would be unfair to Dublin to enter

Strand 2 without a finalized devolution plan from Strand 1. There followed some haggling between Hume and Molyneaux over the degree of depth with which they might later revisit Strand 1 issues in light of Strand 2 developments.

But Mayhew asked that they leave such substantive discussion aside for the moment. He suggested that the next move should be for him to meet each party leader separately and then all together to discuss the state of play as regards both the Sub-Committee report and, in particular, Strand 2. All agreed, and the meeting was adjourned. Hanley talked of a 'businesslike atmosphere' at Stormont, and one of his civil servants identified 'an air of optimism' (*Irish Times* 12 June 1992). There were rumours that at least some SDLP elements were still willing to accept further modifications to their proposal, and the perception was prevalent among Unionists that only Hume had blocked more movement.

Meanwhile, Reynolds and Major held their Rio meeting, where Major made it very clear that the SDLP's Panel proposal was the sticking point. He insisted that not only was it unsellable to Unionism, but it was equally unpalatable to Westminster to accept an EC-appointed member of government within the UK. Reynolds reluctantly agreed to 'give another week for the Northern Ireland parties to decide whether to move on to Strand 2' (ibid.).

For most of that day, and the next morning, Mayhew met with various permutations of the party leaders, trying to agree a joint statement about moving on to Strand 2 talks. On Friday morning, they reconvened the plenary to report on their progress. Molyneaux, on behalf of the four leaders, informed the meeting that they had met (without Mayhew) the previous evening and again that morning, and would be meeting again after the plenary. They hoped to have a report of their discussions for Mayhew soon after that meeting. But the arguments continued throughout the day. Clearly, a simple announcement of the opening of Strand 2 was too much for some Unionists, and for Paisley in particular. He was still insisting that only substantive progress in Strand 1 could permit the move to Strand 2, and that only a finished formula for devolution could constitute such progress. But the pressure from Dublin, and the sense of obligation on the part of the British government to keep their promise to the Irish, worked in the other direction. The compromise that eventually emerged was the idea of holding a 'preliminary' meeting to discuss a Strand 2 agenda, which would represent at least a half-step forward. There were hours of careful negotiation between the leaders, interspersed with internal discussions within the delegations, drafting and redrafting a statement.

Finally, agreement was reached in the late evening to invite Sir Ninian Stephen to convene a preliminary meeting with participants to discuss the Strand 2 agenda, and also to extend the Strand 1 Sub-Committee's life yet again for further work on those aspects of the devolution formula which they had not had time to address. The plenary was reconvened just before 10pm, when Mayhew sought the approval of a statement, drafted by the leaders but phrased in his name, regarding the way forward. The statement's first paragraph read:

> I am not yet proposing the transition to Strand 2. However there is wide agreement on the next steps in the process of the Talks.

But Paisley opened the discussion by saying that, while he himself supported the statement, he had been unable to consult with some senior members of his delegation, and so technically he could not endorse the second sentence. He asked that they suspend the plenary until Monday to allow him to gain the missing delegates' endorsement. But, after a long and argumentative day, the other teams would not accept further delay. Paisley then asked that the second sentence be deleted. The SDLP and Alliance refused. Hume suggested that the problem be resolved by deleting both sentences. Paisley retorted that if the first sentence was removed, he would no longer recommend the statement to his delegation. It was, he insisted, integral to any DUP approval. (Full Strand 2 talks were, after all, one of the greatest symbolic hurdles still awaiting the DUP: engaging directly and formally with the arch-enemy of Dublin.) Hume suggested that the DUP make its own separate statement, since amendments at this plenary stage were unacceptable because they would entail the renegotiation of something already agreed. Mayhew tried to reason with the SDLP, but again they refused to accept alteration. The DUP asked for an adjournment; the Alliance rejected the idea. Paisley again asked what the rush was, suggesting that they await his consultation and reconvene to approve the statement on Monday.

Finally, Mayhew threatened to halt the entire process unless agreement was reached to proceed to Strand 2. He suggested an amendment making it clear that it was his personal judgement – rather than a consensus view among all parties – that there was 'wide agreement' on the next steps. At 10.15pm, this was formally accepted by all. The full statement to plenary was then slightly edited to become a press release, issued at almost midnight:

> The Secretary of State is not yet proposing the transition to Strand II. However it is his judgement that there is wide agreement on the next steps in the process of the Talks. In the light of exchanges between the party leaders, he has asked the Irish government to join with him in inviting Sir Ninian Stephen to convene a meeting next week, to which Sir Ninian would invite representatives of the two governments and of the four Northern Ireland political parties participating in the talks, to discuss a possible agenda for Strand II of the talks. The Secretary of State also proposed that the two governments should hold a meeting in Strand III formation ... to give preliminary consideration to the issues likely to arise in the Strand. In the meantime, he also proposed that the Strand I Sub-Committee should be invited to continue its work on remaining matters. (*Irish Times* 13 June 1992)

Over the weekend, most attention focused on deciding delegates to the preliminary Strand 2 meeting. The UUP nominated Chris McGimpsey and Ken Maginnis, the SDLP Seamus Mallon and Eddie McGrady, and the Alliance Seamus Close and Addie Morrow. The DUP remained silent on the subject, and Dublin announced that they would send only officials, not ministers, to the meeting. But the overall feeling was not a positive one. The SDLP in particular were frustrated. In their view, the Unionists had not only managed to survive for eight weeks of negotiation without talking to Dublin, it appeared that they had also persuaded the British government to accept Articles Two and Three of the Irish constitution on the agenda of Strand 3, when in SDLP eyes they were purely a Strand 2 matter. They suspected that Unionists had agreed to the preliminary Strand 3 meeting primarily to see Britain take the Unionist side over the Articles there without any commitment within Strand 2.

Meanwhile, the four leaders travelled quietly to London on Saturday for separate meetings with Stephen, who was waiting in the Berkeley Hotel for the start of Strand 2. He had been furnished with briefings by both government teams, as well as character sketches of the party leaders. 'The briefings consisted of telling me who the four parties were, who the individual characters in those four parties that I would come across were, and little character sketches of each of them' (Stephen).

'We got the character sketches from both sides,' recalls Thompson:

> Sir Patrick in particular was rather fond of character sketches, but we also got them from the Irish officials. In general, they proved to be pretty accurate, certainly the one of Dr Paisley. On that memorable Saturday morning, Paisley barged into the room larger than life, and more or less his first words after shaking our hands and saying hello were: 'No wining! No dining! No Christian-name calling!' It sounded like a chant: 'No wining! No dining! No Christian-name calling! They're the ground-rules, they're the ground-rules!' That was a bit of a shock, I can tell you. And he lived up to that [when Strand 2 began] – he didn't acknowledge the presence of the Irish team when we ate in the same room, as we did day after day at Stormont.

It was not the most encouraging beginning, in Stephen's view, as the clearly protectionist approaches of the leaders were made manifest to him:

> I think I had a sense of great doubt at those first meetings in London about whether this was actually going to lead anywhere. My feeling was that none of them wished to give a clear indication that this was the beginning of a really worthwhile activity, because that would seem to be a bit of a surrender to the enemy.

With the introductions over, Stephen went back to waiting. 'Mayhew didn't want us to get into discussions with the Northern Ireland parties too soon. He was a bit worried that we might frighten the horses, because he didn't have their agreement to move into Strand 2 yet' (Thompson). But he was well prepared. He had met in London with Mayhew and with Foreign Office and Northern Ireland Office (NIO) officials. In Dublin, he had met with David Andrews, the Irish Foreign Minister, Padraig Flynn, the Irish Justice Minister, and the Irish civil servant team. And his assistant George Thompson had visited Belfast for briefings from the Northern Ireland Office there and from the Anglo-Irish Secretariat. Mayhew made it clear to Stephen that if he did not get agreement to open Strand 2 very soon, he would ask Prime Minister Major to intervene and apply pressure on the Unionists. For his own part, Stephen, as Australian Minister of the Environment, cancelled his visit to the Earth Summit at Rio in order to keep the way clear for Strand 2.

4

'Strand One-and-a-Half': June

British and Irish officials met in Dublin on Monday 15 June to discuss the Strand 2 preliminary meeting, and the agenda for the intergovernmental Strand 3 meeting. Behind the scenes they had, over the previous fortnight, hammered out some of the procedural details of Strand 2 with Thompson and Stephen. Their formal announcement after the meeting indicated that the 'pre-Strand 2 meeting' would be held in London, on Wednesday or Friday, and that Strand 3 was likely to happen the following week, probably in London. The vagueness over the dates reflected a tension between the two governments. London was keen to press on with the process. But Dublin, for all its insistence on opening Strand 2, was dealing with a heavy schedule of European and other matters, and was having trouble finding time.

The DUP, for their part, publicly declared their preconditions for the meetings: they would attend only if Articles Two and Three were on the Strand 3 agenda and if they got assurances that Strand 2 would not open fully until a devolution structure had been agreed in Strand 1. That day, Paisley wrote at greater length to Mayhew:

> The only reason for the proposal to have an informal meeting ... was on the request of Mr Hume. He stated that if, on the agenda for Strand 2, there was to be an opportunity for him to ascertain whether he would be able to deal with his problems of identity, then he would be able to withdraw his reservations on the document that other parties agreed for institutions of government within Northern Ireland ... The unionists were keen to have

Strand III commenced so that for their part they could see clearly demonstrated the attitude of HMG to Articles 2 & 3 of the Republic's constitution and the South's intention to try and destroy the Union.

The DUP had still not announced who of their number might actually attend the meetings. When Jeremy Hanley declared that he fully intended to be at the Strand 2 preliminary meeting, questions arose over the previous Irish announcement that it would be attended by officials only and not ministers.

Meanwhile, the Strand 1 Sub-Committee resumed their conversations. After their dramas of recent weeks, their work now was much less contentious. They discussed the topics they had not yet covered, and by close of business on Tuesday they submitted two more papers: a very detailed one on possible processes of public finance for the new institutions in the North, and another lengthy one entitled *Human Rights, a Bill of Rights, and Cultural Expression and Diversity*.

On Tuesday, Ninian Stephen arrived in Dublin to meet with the Irish and British civil servant teams. At the same time, his invitations to the preliminary Strand 2 meeting were received: it would take place on Friday in London, with provision for an extension into the weekend if needed. Alliance, the SDLP and the UUP confirmed their attendance, the latter on the condition that the meeting was strictly confined to setting an agenda. The DUP stayed silent, still waiting for the assurances they had requested, beyond saying that their participants would be low-level to reflect the unimportance of the meeting. The Irish government confirmed on Wednesday that they would send only officials. Late on Thursday night, the DUP finally announced that they had received the assurances they needed and would thus be sending Rhonda Paisley (the leader's daughter), Nigel Dodds and Simpson Gibson to the next day's meeting of 'Strand One-and-a-half' (*Irish Times* 19 June 1992).

In the event, the meeting passed off 'wholly uneventfully' (*Irish Times* 22 June 1992) on Friday 19 June. Each government and party offered an opening statement which included a suggested agenda. Giving the DUP statement, Nigel Dodds quoted heavily from Paisley's letter to Mayhew, and once again declared the intention of placing centrally on the agenda 'the illegal claim of the Irish

Republic in its constitution to the territory of part of Her Majesty's United Kingdom, namely Northern Ireland'. For the UUP, Ken Maginnis laid out a long set of procedural, terminological and other assurances which they sought (and received) from Stephen. The agenda was discussed at length, and finally a composite version was tabled by Stephen. All the parties agreed, excepting the DUP, who reserved their position on it. Indeed, the Australian facilitators detected growing tension within the DUP between pro- and anti-talks factions. There still remained a degree of fudge about the position of the Irish Articles Two and Three and the British Government of Ireland Act in the projected discussions. But perhaps the meeting's greatest significance was that, although Ireland was represented only at the level of government officials, the meeting broke the symbolic bar on Unionists talking directly with an Irish government. It was also agreed that the preliminary Strand 3 meeting should happen the following week.

Over the weekend, Stephen sent invitations to the party leaders to join him in further informal preparatory meetings the following Friday, while Dublin and the SDLP continued to increase the pressure to have Strand 2 formally opened within a week. Indeed, during the week ahead, no formal Strand 1 business was done at Stormont. Instead, increasingly unseemly wrangles developed over the other Strands. Paisley opened the bidding with a public statement (the first from any party since the press embargo was instituted at the beginning of Strand 1) criticizing the Irish government for delaying the preliminary Strand 3 meeting which Britain had hoped to hold the next day. (Paisley was keen to see the meeting take place, hoping that it would engage the British government in a debate opposing Irish views on Articles Two and Three and force them to express their preference for Strand 1 completion before full engagement in Strand 2. He could then quote a 'British position' on such matters.) A day later, David Trimble of the UUP joined the criticism of the Irish government, who claimed still to be in preliminary discussions about the Strand 3 meeting, despite British urgency on the matter. And Alderdice also released a statement criticising Dublin for 'stalling the momentum' of the process and putting 'the whole process in jeopardy' (*Irish Times* 25 June 1992).

In fact, a considerable row was brewing between the governments.

Britain wanted the meeting held that week, and at ministerial level. Ireland preferred to keep it at the level of officials, and refused to open Strand 3 fully until Strand 2 was in full operation. Dublin believed that Unionists wanted Strand 3 open so that the British could 'take Dublin on' over the Articles, and refused in return to engage in such debate until Unionists had committed themselves fully to Strand 2. To do otherwise, they argued, would be to allow the Unionists to 'pole-vault' over Strand 2 into Strand 3 (*Irish Times* 25 June 1992). The initial date for the meeting was Wednesday 24 June, but at the last minute the Irish team announced that they were not yet ready. In fact, they feared that the meeting would permit the Unionists to place the matter of change to Articles Two and Three so early in the Strand 3 agenda that it would effectively become a precondition for progress on any other issues in that strand.

On Thursday, Mayhew openly blamed the Irish government for the Strand 3 delay, announcing in the Commons that he was 'sorry the Irish government could not agree' to meet this week. Albert Reynolds responded, from the EC summit in Lisbon, that 'there was never any request [from the British] for a meeting, and I repeat, never.' The Irish government, he declared, was 'ready and waiting' for Strand 2 to begin (*Irish Times* 26 June 1992). He went on to criticize both Paisley and Alderdice for breaking confidentiality by releasing their statements. Meanwhile, the two civil servant teams had been discussing arrangements for the pre-Strand 3 meeting, expected within a week, and their report to the Taoiseach convinced Reynolds to raise the profile of the meeting by sending David Andrews rather than just officials. After the summit in Lisbon, Reynolds met with Major to confirm details, and they announced that the pre-Strand 3 meeting would take place the following Tuesday in London. The decision to send the Irish Foreign Minister to the meeting dramatically raised the profile of the event – since Northern Ireland parties would attend, it thus being the first direct formal constitutional discussion between Unionist politicians and the Irish government since the 1920s – and effectively put the pressure back on Mayhew to open Strand 2 promptly. Indeed, Reynolds's belief that his concession on Strand 3 would win gains on Strand 2 was explicit in his statement to the press on Friday that the decision was designed 'to clear the way for Sir Patrick Mayhew to proceed and call Strand 2 talks' (*Irish Times*

30 June 1992).

While the intergovernmental argument seemed to have been resolved, other disagreements continued. Dublin and the SDLP maintained that the following Tuesday's pre-Strand 3 meeting was an agenda-setting exercise only, and would be followed by a swift announcement of a Strand 2 opening. The DUP claimed that the meeting would be much more substantive, and their opportunity to see the Irish government's negotiating hand. Over the weekend, the arguments continued. Despite Strand 2 now being at least four weeks behind schedule, Paisley declared it was still 'very, very far away ... This [Strand 3] meeting has nothing to do with Strand 2, and everyone knows that except Albert Reynolds' (*Irish Times* 30 June 1992). The SDLP in turn was annoyed at Mayhew for, in their eyes, letting the Unionists have their way.

In the event, the pre-Strand 3 meeting took place at the Queen Elizabeth II Conference Centre in London, on Tuesday 30 June. The meeting lasted two hours, a significant part of it being taken up with a long diatribe by Paisley on history, terrorism, the failures of Dublin, Articles Two and Three, the vacillation of British governments, and so on (*Irish Times* 7 July 1992). David Trimble joined in, declaring that the 'irredentist attitudes enshrined in Articles Two and Three ... are contrary to the accepted principles of international law' (*Irish Times* 8 July 1992). Following the meeting, both governments said they had agreed 'a framework for substantive discussion in Strand Three of the talks, including an agenda' (*Irish Times* 1 July 1992). Andrews declared that he was 'now looking forward to beginning Strand 2 as quickly as possible', while Mayhew contented himself with a brief 'let's wait and see' (ibid.).

Back at Stormont on Wednesday morning, 1 July, Mayhew and Hanley held a series of meetings with the party leaders, pushing hard for agreement to open the other Strands. Hume was strong in support of the move, offering two short SDLP papers setting out the necessity of doing so. Other party leaders were less enthusiastic, and Paisley in particular set out some requirements he would need before agreeing. He and Molyneaux had been demanding for some time that Mayhew offer an official British point of view on the four devolution proposals. In contrast, the SDLP (and Dublin) argued that Britain was an impartial chair in Strand 1, where it could only express neutral opinions, and could only become a player representing and expressing British interests when Strands 2 and 3 opened. Additionally, the Unionist leaders sought a statement of position from the British government on the unequivocal constitutional status of Northern Ireland within the UK.

In the afternoon, Mayhew called a plenary, where he offered a draft of an official statement on the opening of Strands 2 and 3. The statement incorporated some of Hume's earlier points, and Mayhew offered additional comments at the meeting to satisfy Paisley. With an agreement to permit Stephen and the Dublin government to see the recent papers from Strand 1, and despite some last-minute SDLP sniping at Paisley for breaking the press embargo with his remarks at the weekend about Reynolds and the Irish government, the text of the statement was agreed within half an hour, and attached to the official record of the meeting. The plenary was then adjourned. The final text of Mayhew's statement to plenary reviewed progress to date, as well as offering, for Paisley's particular benefit, a strong flavour of British opinion on Strand 1 matters:

> It is clear we are not collectively able to move towards a greater degree of consensus on new political institutions for Northern Ireland at this stage. It is, however, my judgement that developments in other strands of the talks would enable one party or another to shift its position and enable further progress towards full agreement on arrangements for the government of Northern Ireland ...
>
> HMG, for its part, would be willing to facilitate the implementation of the institutional arrangements outlined in the Sub-Committee report of 10 June, including those aspects not at present universally agreed if, but only if, they came in light of further exchanges in the Talks, whether in Strand I or in other strands, to attract the support of all four parties ...
>
> I can say on behalf of the [British] government that unless and until the four parties agree on a different approach, we take the view that discussions in Strand II could be expected to take place on the premise that any new political institutions in Northern Ireland would be based on the structures outlined in the Sub-Committee report. The government is ready to enter and participate in discussions in Strand II on that basis ...
>
> I believe it is in everyone's interest that the Talks process as a

whole should achieve an unambiguous consensus on the constitutional position of Northern Ireland, and produce a framework
for relationships which will be genuinely acceptable to all the
Talks participants ... That may have implications for Articles 2
and 3 of the Irish constitution ...

My conclusion is that there is no more work that can usefully
be done in Strand I at present, though in due course there
certainly will be, and that the most constructive route forward is
to build on the work done in the preparatory meetings for
Strands II and III and to move forward now into those strands of
discussion. I therefore now formally propose that the later
strands of discussion should be launched. I do so with the agreement of each of the party leaders.

In public, Mayhew's subsequent press statement merely noted
that he was proposing to launch Strands 2 and 3, and that 'in the
light of points made by the Secretary of State during consultation
and in plenary, the party leaders indicated that they accepted the
proposal'. Announcing his decision to the press at 6pm, Mayhew
declared it was 'the best moment so far' (*Irish Times* 2 July 1992).

The expectation now was that Strand 2 would swing into action
very swiftly. Indeed, the parties received Stephen's invitation to
talks the following morning. Strand 2 would run for three days of
next week at Lancaster House in London, then for three days of the
following week at Stormont, and then for three more days of a third
week in Dublin. It was immediately obvious that such a schedule
would take the talks to 22 July, just five days before the deadline of
the scheduled Anglo-Irish Conference. Already, Reynolds was
hinting that an extension of negotiating time – a postponement of
the Conference – was a possibility.

5
Strand 2:
'Tension on Demand': July

Sir Ninian Stephen convened the first meeting of Strand 2 at 2pm on Monday 6 July, in the Music Room of Lancaster House in London. He sat at the head of the table, with his assistant, the Australian civil servant George Thompson. On their left sat the Alliance delegation (Alderdice, Close, Morrow and Neeson), then the Irish government representatives (Andrews, John Wilson, the Tanaiste and Minister of Defence, Padraig Flynn, Minister of Justice, and Bobby Molloy, the Energy Minister who was standing in for Des O'Malley, the leader of the Progressive Democrats and Minister for Industry and Commerce), and finally the SDLP (Hume, Mallon, McGrady and Hendron). To Stephen's immediate right sat the UUP delegates (Molyneaux, Nicholson, Maginnis and Chris McGimpsey), then the British government (Mayhew, Hanley, John Chilcott, the Permanent Under-Secretary at the NIO, and David Fell, the head of the Northern Ireland Civil Service), and beside them the DUP (Paisley, Robinson, James McClure and Simpson Gibson). Even the seating was a matter for negotiation, as Stephen recalled:

> One of the great problems was trying to determine where people could sit, and how you might insulate them from each other. There was a strong insistence on the part of the Unionists that they not be next to the Irish. And the Ulster Unionists didn't want to be next to Paisley's group. So we had to have the British as a sort of buffer between the two, then the SDLP next to Paisley, then the Irish ministers, and then Alliance. This took a lot of time to work out.

Stephen opened the proceedings with a statement on his own behalf. In particular, he laid out his understanding of his own role:

> I regard my function as simply that of chairing meetings, whether plenary or in committee, my aim being to ensure, with the guidance of the Business Committee ... that everything possible is done to assist you in your discussions and that no procedural obstacles are allowed to obstruct that aim; exclusively a facilitating role, in which I shall seek assistance from all of you. I may from time to time make procedural suggestions and I accept responsibility for procedural arrangements; but procedure, like substance, is ultimately a matter for the parties.

He also outlined his view of how the talks process might proceed. Working from the agenda they had previously designed, he hoped that initial discussions would:

> assist in reducing to an agreed text whatever areas there are of substantial agreement between the parties. We could then move from there to the margins of agreement, extending the scope of agreement until areas of unequivocal disagreement are defined. Then the task may prove to be one of finding ways around those areas. All this will obviously involve a deal of work, much of it probably best done in small working groups.

His suggested timetable for this first three-day plenary involved opening statements on Monday and Tuesday. Wednesday would then be for discussion, questioning and clarification of the statements, with a short period reserved at the end for nominations to a Business Committee (one member from each delegation). Further sessions, he suggested, might

> begin with a, perhaps quite brief, plenary session to decide the order of work and the subjects usefully to be referred to working groups ... Each group can work through its allotted subject matter and report back ... I would contemplate chairing each of these working groups, none of them being held simultaneously.

Following Stephen's introduction, Wilson read out a joint

message of goodwill from Reynolds and Major. Then Mayhew gave a progress report on Strand 1. There was some disagreement over how then to proceed, and eventually Stephen won agreement to have all the opening statements presented in series before any questioning of them. The delegations would present in order: Alliance, Ireland, the SDLP, Britain, the UDUP (as the DUP often referred to itself in the talks, prefacing its usual title with an extra Ulster), and finally the UUP.

And so business began with Alderdice's opening statement. As with all the statements, there was much rhetoric about the importance of the talks, the responsibility on the delegates, and so on, but Alderdice's words were largely addressed to the Irish government. He did not miss the opportunity to raise Articles Two and Three as a key issue, and to remind the Irish delegation that 'if you see these talks ... as some kind of back door to a United Ireland, you are dreaming dreams which can make a real relationship difficult if not impossible'. Instead, he suggested a focus on establishing joint North–South commissions to develop co-operation in areas of common interest, and a Tripartite Council to help manage the North–South–British axis. It occurred to one SDLP participant that Alderdice had given the presentation of 'a polite Unionist'.

In turn, Wilson read the Irish government's substantial opening statement. He stated his belief that accommodation between the traditions was an inevitable reality sooner or later, wondering more simply 'whether we here can achieve this necessary goal, or whether we will pass the problem on unresolved ... Today's meeting ... is a recognition that we will never solve our problems by denying each other's existence.' The statement was a wide-ranging summary of official Irish attitudes to the North and to Anglo-Irish history, and defined the problem as one of conflicting rights. But implicitly Wilson challenged the Unionist view of the conflict and, indeed, of the whole remit of the negotiations:

> The poles of the problem we are called upon to resolve are not between two rival views of how Northern Ireland should be governed within the UK. There have been many attempts to redefine the problem in these more manageable terms, and they have all failed. The poles of the problem are between those who resent the very existence of Northern Ireland, and those who see

its existence, and its British status, as vital for their identity.

To the annoyance of Unionists around the table, he went on to paraphrase one of the deeply held tenets of SDLP reasoning: that parity of esteem was essential, but that equally essential was the practical expression of it in structures that reflected the equal involvement of both traditions. He closed by setting out clearly Dublin's expectations for progress:

> The Anglo-Irish Agreement was ... a formal acceptance that the Irish government have both a concern and a role in relation to Northern Ireland. We would expect that any broader agreement which might be reached would incorporate these elements in full measure. Otherwise, something of value would be lost.

While hardly unexpected, the statement was a challenge to the Unionist position: where they had entered the talks with the goal of smashing the Agreement, Dublin was insisting from the start that building upon the Agreement represented the minimum requirement and would be pursued 'in full measure'.

After Wilson, it was Hume's turn. Again, there was very little to surprise in his words, but he did take the opportunity to stress the SDLP's belief that Strand 2 was 'the most important of all the discussions that are taking place in these talks', and that any overall agreement they might reach would need endorsement by simultaneous referendums in North and South.

Finally, for the day, Mayhew gave the British statement. His opening words demonstrated the dual position in which the Secretary of State now found himself:

> I enter Strand 2 as a participant rather than as Chairman. Yet it continues to be as important to me to facilitate agreement as to argue my own corner. Her Majesty's Government has obligations and responsibilities which are relevant to the Strand 2 discussions. But it has no blueprint of its own for Strand 2.

But as he went on, his words must have sounded a slight encouragement to Unionist hearts, as they offered an indirect challenge to Wilson's earlier words. An overall outcome, he hoped:

should enable all participants to acknowledge Northern Ireland's present status as a part of the UK, and to recognise that there will be no change in that status without the consent of a majority of the people who live there, [and] that the present wish of a majority is for no change ...

In words reminiscent of his final statement to the Strand 1 plenary, he suggested that this would have implications for Articles Two and Three, and welcomed an earlier assurance by Reynolds that the Articles would be 'on the table' during the talks. Indeed he then went on to quote his plenary statement to the effect that, until something better came along, it was the British assumption that a Strand 1 solution would be in essence the structures outlined in the Sub-Committee report, whatever the SDLP's dissent from it.

The day at an end, Stephen postponed the Unionist statements until the following morning. But Tuesday's session opened with another wrangle over procedural matters, Unionists wanting to start questioning the statements so far presented, the others insisting that they complete all the opening statements before questioning began. Stephen understood such nervous fretting over details:

I was expecting that kind of thing, and it didn't come as any surprise. I realised that these people had a lot potentially to lose if the impression should get out that they were giving in too easily. So everything had to be hard bargaining.

The procedure agreed on Monday prevailed, but before Paisley could begin, Haughey and Alderdice raised the matter of press leaks. That morning's *Irish Times* had carried excerpts from the minutes of the previous week's pre-Strand 3 meeting, in particular critical statements made by both Paisley and Alderdice and directed towards the Irish government. As ever, accusations and denials flew around the room, and all responsibility was denied. But strong suspicions remained that it had been in DUP interests to release evidence that Paisley, in particular, was battling as strongly as ever against the old foe. This was followed by various complaints about the DUP's habit of calling itself the UDUP in the talks process as a mechanism to ensure that when alphabetical order was used, their turn always came after the Irish government and the SDLP, and guaranteed that both Unionist parties were heard together and last.

Amidst such an antagonistic mood, Paisley rose in combative style to give his opening statement. 'I got to like Paisley,' recalled Stephen. 'He was a great character, a marvellous producer of tension on demand.' The DUP leader began by spelling out that his party was only present because Mayhew had expressly accepted that the Strand 1 *Possible Outline Framework* – despite SDLP dissent – formed the basis of a Strand 1 model of sufficient substance to allow progress to Strand 2. The long paper that followed contained few surprises. Warning all that 'issues must be raised, even if they cut raw nerves. Dancing around the subject cannot aid us', he launched into a lengthy review of the history of the Irish Republic. Inevitably, his argument centred on the 'illegal, criminal and immoral claim' of Articles Two and Three, and on the Anglo-Irish Agreement. Quoting Mayhew and other British ministers in support, he insisted that the Union was not up for debate in these talks, and that the aim of Strand 2 was for North and South to develop as 'good neighbours'.

There was a coffee break, and then Maginnis presented the UUP statement. It was equally lengthy, and offered a similar, if perhaps more erudite, critique of the Irish constitution. Maginnis asserted that, despite nationalist demands for 'parity of esteem', in fact 'the political reality of Irish Nationalism is one which denies legitimacy to the Irish Unionist tradition'. Moreover, he warned the Irish government, 'failure to recognise that those who support and desire the continuance of the Union will never consent to any process or settlement which would precipitate movement towards a United Ireland, is … a fundamental error.' A long textual criticism of Articles Two and Three followed, ending with the assertion that no overall settlement was achievable without their alteration:

> We serve notice now, under the rule that 'nothing is agreed until everything is agreed', that we will not enter into any arrangements whilst the Republic's harsh, irredentist and uncompromising territorial claim is extant.

When Maginnis finished, Stephen asked that they nominate delegates to the Business Committee, which then met during the lunch break to agree dates, times and venues for Strand 2 sessions beyond this week. After lunch, the procedural argument about questioning of statements erupted again. Andrews asked that all questions to the Irish delegation be noted and responded to en bloc. Paisley and the UUP preferred that responses be given question by question, but they lost the argument. Eventually, Stephen called on Alderdice to take questions on his statement. This took the meeting through most of the afternoon, and then they turned briefly to procedural matters. They agreed to adjourn this first round of talks at lunchtime the next day, to resume at Stormont a week later. Finally, there was some argument about the date of the impending Conference meeting, currently scheduled for about three weeks' time. The SDLP suggested that they take an early summer break before then and reconvene in Belfast in September, while the Unionists argued for an extension of the talks deadline into August. Behind the apparently trivial row was the continual attack by Unionists on the Anglo-Irish Conference meeting which would signal the end of negotiations: if they could win a postponement of the meeting, they could claim (whatever the realities) to be weakening further the workings of the Agreement. However, the two governments promised a response on the matter by next week's resumption. And after agreeing a terse press release, they adjourned until the following morning.

Wednesday morning began with another series of complaints of press leaks. The *Irish Times'* indefatigable (and former UUP party official) Frank Millar had got hold of a copy of the Strand 1 *Possible Outline Framework* and of Mayhew's opening Strand 2 address, both of which were quoted extensively in the morning paper. Stephen promised that if it happened again he would issue a press release designed to deter further leaks.

The rest of the morning was entirely taken up with 'lengthy and robust' (*Irish Times* 9 July 1992) cross-examination of the Irish government by all four parties. Wilson and Andrews fielded the questions, which included intense Unionist interrogation over Articles Two and Three, particularly by Paisley. Much of his attack centred on the question of whether the Articles expressed an aspiration or a constitutional imperative to unity. The Irish delegation was somewhat uncomfortable on the matter, and tried to deflect the questions, but Maginnis weighed in with support for Paisley. The argument widened to include the Helsinki Accords, and the semantic difference between 'immutable' and 'inviolable'. Stephen intervened to say that they were entering a negotiation phase prematurely, and asked delegates to revert to questions of clarification. Mallon tried valiantly to support Andrews and Wilson through the onslaught, but it was something of a baptism of fire, the Irish ministers' first real introduction to a confrontational process that the Northern politicians had been engaging in for much longer than they had. Moreover, Paisley's aggressive tactics proved very effective in provoking them, Andrews in particular at this stage, as Thompson noticed:

> Andrews was quick-tempered, and he didn't really have his temper under control in the early stages. But he was obviously deeply committed, and I think he's a man of deep convictions. I had some interesting private conversations with him in a social capacity, and I was quite impressed by him. But he was too quick-tempered in the talks process.

Time ran out before the questioning was finished. The Business Committee reported to the plenary that talks would continue for at least two days of the following week in Belfast. It was becoming very clear that there might have to be several weeks' more talking in Belfast before they could hope to hold a concluding session in Dublin, and also that the overall talks deadline of late July could not be maintained. Nonetheless, the Australian facilitators were upbeat. 'At the outset, there was all this rhetoric about commitment to the process, and we generally believed all the parties were quite genuine in their commitment. We did quite firmly believe that there was a possibility of coming out with a general agreement' (Thompson).

It had been a tough first round in Strand 2, especially for the Irish delegation. Thompson noted their reception:

> First of all, the Irish team weren't expecting quite that degree of antipathy, that strength of feeling across the table, the invective that was hurled at them. And being ministers of a sovereign state I think they found it very, very hard to take. I don't think they ever recognised the Ulster Unionists – or the DUP – as equal players in the process, which made it harder for them to stomach

the sort of treatment they were given. The days of grilling by Paisley and Robinson and others about their opening presentation must have been immensely frustrating ... They were guilty sometimes of churlishness in the way they responded to that, but I always found their attitude understandable.

On a lighter note, it emerged that Seamus Mallon had passed around a successful racing tip. One source estimated joint Irish/SDLP winnings at around £2000, while Mayhew had put £10 on the winner. The DUP took no part in such gambling practice, and the UUP's Ken Maginnis was disappointed that he missed out, and 'highly suspicious of this clandestine passage of information between the SDLP, Irish and British delegations ... Unionists would be happy to share in those things of benefit to the whole community' (*Irish Times* 11 July 1992).

Unionist participants travelled back from London to prepare for the Orange marches of the Twelfth weekend. At the traditional speeches, Molyneaux criticized the SDLP for 'wanting holidays' instead of prolonging the talks deadline, and indulging in 'endless dissertations over political philosophy (*Irish Times* 14 July 1992), while Paisley predictably attacked the 'immoral claim' of Articles Two and Three (ibid.). Meanwhile, Stephen, his wife and Thompson transferred their base to the Culloden Hotel on the shores of Belfast Lough. 'We were put up in splendid accommodation. We certainly couldn't complain about that. It was just the isolation that got us down after a while' (Thompson).

The following Wednesday, Strand 2 reconvened at Stormont. The Business Committee met at 10am to set procedures for the week. Talks would be held all day Wednesday and Thursday, and on Friday morning. The plenary opened at 11am, and the Business Committee reported that they had been unable to set arrangements beyond the current week because of the continuing uncertainty over the date of the Anglo-Irish Conference meeting, and would meet again at 5pm, following the plenary.

The entire day was then taken up with continued questions to the Irish government delegation, with O'Malley now reinstated in the team. Alderdice led the Alliance team in a prolonged examination of the Irish statement, before Robinson pounced on the question of the status of Northern Ireland. He demanded that the Irish define that status, but Andrews and Flynn refused to go beyond expressions of support for the Agreement. 'Every time the Anglo-Irish Agreement was mentioned, it was like a sword plunged into Paisley's heart,' Stephen observed. 'The mere mention of it would start him off.' Tempers were raised. 'They would shout at one another, and from time to time it became quite heated,' he recalled. 'And all I had to do was to shout a bit louder.' Again, Mallon tried to turn the inquisition on Robinson, but Paisley trained the guns back on the Republic, its history, the definitions of nationalism and republicanism, and the sniping and defending pattern continued until lunch.

The afternoon session began with a request from a disgruntled Alderdice that the Business Committee do something to improve the service in the Stormont restaurant, and then the DUP attack continued, on the interpretation of history, the role of the Irish diaspora, the validity of the New Ireland Forum, whether Britain stole the North from Ireland or Ireland stole the Republic from Britain and, of course, the Agreement and the Articles. Thus the day was completed. With the cross-examinations proceeding so slowly, it was unlikely that they would finish before the end of Friday's session, and with the Conference deadline now just two weeks away, a decision was going to have to be made soon about an extension or postponement. Outside, Stormont was shrouded in mist all day; inside, the talks remained shrouded in secrecy. When the Irish delegation came out for a photocall in the afternoon, they remained tight-lipped and unforthcoming. One NIO official deigned to inform the assembled press that the room inside was crowded, that the table was of mahogany, and that there were three clocks in the room. He did not mention that an anonymous Unionist graffiti artist had modified a sign in the cloakroom to read 'Articles 2 and 3 Left At Owners' Risk'. No one else was talking at all, and the media had to settle for watching the indefatigable lone unionist, Cedric Wilson, continuing his unending anti-negotiation protest outside the building. The Business Committee met briefly in the evening, but made no progress on the future programme of work.

The questioning of the Irish delegation continued all day Thursday, as Unionists maintained the interrogation over Articles Two and Three, border security, church–state relations in the

Republic, and so on. From time to time, the Irish ministers fell back on the defence that this was a discussion phase of the talks, aimed at identifying the issues for negotiation, rather than the negotiation itself. But the DUP mission to score points and find holes in the Irish arguments was relentless. Stephen intervened to see if he could bring the questioning to an end, but the Unionists were not interested. They challenged the Irish ministers to defend the Republic against the charge that the Protestant minority there had suffered discrimination since partition. Andrews and O'Malley tried to move the conversation away from religious terms, claiming that the Republic no longer thought in those categories, but the Unionists had prepared their Irish history well, and were not short of ammunition.

Mallon eventually intervened in the afternoon on a 'point of order' to warn that many around the table were approaching a boredom threshold, and to ask for an acceleration of the process. Paisley responded that he was, as usual, asking short questions, and that he was there to be open and frank and to do a job for his people. Once again, he put the Irish on the defensive over the constitution. He quoted past statements by O'Malley that Articles Two and Three were 'no use to nationalism', and that the Irish constitution was approved in referendum by 'only a small majority, with no one in the North consulted'. And then he challenged Andrews to agree. The unrelenting Unionist pressure forced O'Malley (a Progressive Democrat, and the only non-Fianna Fail minister present that day) into admitting that his party's current preference was to change unilaterally Articles Two and Three. This contrasted sharply with stated Fianna Fail policy, which was to accept any such change only in tandem with alterations to Britain's Government of Ireland Act. 'It was pretty clear all through,' commented Stephen, 'that there was a tension between [the Irish delegation] . . . You didn't feel that any one of them could speak for the whole delegation in quite the same way that Mayhew could.' 'It wasn't a unified delegation,' agrees Thompson. Paisley finally rested, happy to have driven a wedge among the Irish team on such a core concern.

On Friday morning, Vitty, McClure and Dodds took over the DUP attack, securing acknowledgement from the Irish delegation that they were enthusiastic about, but reserved their position on, the

SDLP proposal for a Dublin-sponsored Commission or Panel member in a Strand 1 settlement. The morning's tactic was one of trying to find divisions between Dublin and the SDLP. Finally, the discussions moved on from the Irish statement, and before lunch Hume took questions on his, initially from Alliance, and then from the Irish delegation. The afternoon session began with a brief argument about Strand 3. Mayhew and Andrews announced that they intended to hold the first full Strand 3 meeting in the week beginning 27 July. Mayhew noted that, unlike the preliminary Strand 3 meeting, this time they did not envisage inviting any observers from the Northern parties. Nicholson complained that the UUP wanted time and opportunity to make a presentation at that meeting, as Alliance and the DUP had done at the pre-Strand 3 meeting. Alderdice expressed surprise that they hadn't taken the opportunity then. Mayhew promised that the opportunity would be made available at some later point. Then Stephen moved the focus back to Strand 2, and the Irish questioning of Hume continued until mid-afternoon.

After that, Mayhew answered questions on his own statement. In particular, he faced some insistent questioning from the DUP regarding his readiness to endorse the Strand 1 structures to which the SDLP had not agreed, and he agreed that Britain's first priority in deciding whether or not to support a solution would be according to its endorsement by all Northern parties, rather than to its actual content. The DUP tactic, once again, was to try to drive wedges between Mayhew and his Irish counterparts. But Mayhew played a close game, repeatedly drawing his answers from the *Common Themes* and *Common Principles* documents. Stephen closed the day's session with an announcement that there would be three more plenary days the following week in Belfast, and that by the first of those days, arrangements concerning the Conference meeting and the first Strand 3 meeting would have been resolved.

Over the weekend, Irish ministers defended themselves against accusations of a split in their delegation over the question of changing Articles Two and Three, and in turn joined the SDLP in blaming Unionists for leaking copies of the Irish opening statement. One SDLP delegate complained about the drip-drip style of leaking, and wished that they could stick to the rule that, 'nothing shall be leaked until everything is leaked' (*Irish Times* 22 July 1992).

As the plenary resumed on Wednesday 22 July, Stephen reported from the previous day's Business Committee that the initial Strand 3 meeting would definitely be held during the following week. The talks would then take a recess until September, since a postponement of the Conference meeting was now unavoidable. In this way, all three Strands would have at least opened before the original Conference deadline, and Strand 2 could resume in September by getting to substantive negotiations.

Leaks and matters of confidentiality were then addressed again. It was beginning to look fairly obvious that the leaks had issued from Unionist sources, especially since the gist of the leaked stories concerned rifts between members of the Irish delegation, and between Dublin and the SDLP. The Unionists defended themselves, Molyneaux accusing the NIO of the leaks, and Paisley branding the journalist in question a 'well-known Republican'. Stephen took full note of the strongly expressed concerns of all the delegations, and introduced a paper on strict procedures for the handling, copying and dissemination of documents. Then, mindful of his promise at the time of the last leak, at the close of the day's business he issued a press release claiming unanimity among all participants in condemning the leaks, and offering some harsh criticisms of those responsible:

> All six parties to these talks today joined in denouncing the so-called 'leaks' that occurred ... The 'leaks' are not only inaccurate and misleading, but also put the whole talks process in jeopardy. They come from tainted sources, from people who blithely disregard their undertaking to observe confidentiality and put personal or political advantage above the common good. (*Irish Times* 23 July 1992)

Recalling the events later, Stephen accepts that the leaks may have been less disruptive than the attention paid to them would indicate, but that for the sake of form, he felt obliged to release such critical statements:

> One had to assume that it was very serious, and say, 'Don't they realise they're jeopardising the talks?' But whether it was really doing that I don't know. I think no one was really very surprised

about it. So many things do leak. They were all politicians ... and they must have played the game of using the media to their advantage for years. So I think it was an opportunity to make a point, make a stand. But I don't know if it really was so important.

In the day's plenary session, cross-examination of the British opening statement concluded in time for Mayhew to leave for Westminster. Then Paisley faced questions on his own statement, including a 'line by line grilling' by the Irish and the SDLP in revenge for his interrogations of the previous week (*Irish Times* 23 July 1992). Stephen intervened to point out that they were arguing over history and seemed to be needlessly irritating one another: was it necessary, he queried? Wilson doggedly insisted it was a necessary process of identifying errors in the DUP analysis, and the grilling went on.

Eventually, as the temperatures continued to rise in the room, Paisley declared that Articles Two and Three were a 'Berlin Wall' in the situation. If they were out of the way, a range of new possibilities would emerge, but if there was to be no change in them, then there was no point to the DUP's continuing presence. As Andrews countered that no delegation could promise such a move in advance of an entire negotiated settlement, Paisley declared that he was not prepared to take a Dublin government's word on trust. Flynn accused him of setting preconditions. Paisley insisted he was not, but that there could be no settlement without alteration of the Articles: the Irish government must give a commitment that it would change its constitution before any progress could be made in the talks. Tempers flared, and breakdown looked a possibility. Stephen called a 25-minute recess to let tensions cool.

But there was no progress on the point. On his return to the table, Paisley accused the Irish of questioning the integrity of the DUP delegation. Flynn declared his delegation was under no obligation to give any commitment to anyone. Paisley complained that the Irish were patronizing Northern Ireland. Flynn objected to hearing Articles Two and Three described with expletives. Then, in a calculated insult, he described Northern Ireland, quoting a famous remark by former Taoiseach Charles Haughey, as 'a failed political entity since 1920'. Paisley replied that it was easy for anyone in the

South to make these remarks, and highly insulting.

Stephen drew the increasingly fractious day to a close with a report from that morning's Business Committee, where it had been agreed that Strand 3 would meet in Dublin the following Tuesday, and that the Conference meeting scheduled for July would not now take place before 28 September. This latter decision represented a considerable sop to Unionists, who would of course walk out as soon as any Conference meeting signalled the return to operation of the Agreement, but a worry for Dublin (and the SDLP to some extent) who saw it as a continuing erosion of the Agreement in return for little or no substantive progress in negotiations.

On Thursday, the Irish interrogation of Paisley continued, as tense as before. Paisley accused previous Irish governments of trying to eliminate their Protestant population. Andrews enquired about the security of Free Presbyterian churches in the Republic. Paisley complained that they had had windows broken. As they moved back on to the referendum argument, Flynn asked would Paisley interfere in any Southern referendum. Paisley said no. Would his actions have any influence on a referendum? Paisley accepted they might have some effect. Then Flynn asked would Paisley assist the Irish government in the referendum. Paisley hotly replied that he did not assist thieves. There was uproar, and Stephen intervened to congratulate Flynn for not responding to such a comment.

The topic moved on to the Ulster Defence Regiment, but the quality of debate remained the same. Mercifully, lunchtime intervened. The morning was a typical illustration of the personality clashes – between three personalities in particular – with which Stephen had to deal:

> Andrews was very much the lawyer, seemed to be the lawyer speaking. But he could fire up and become quite strong-minded about things, and do a bit of banging on the table ...
>
> Flynn was the sort of archetypal Irishman in a way, and he seemed to irritate others around the table more than anyone. He was a very beguiling and amusing character, but I think the Unionists regarded him as typical of their enemy to the South ...
>
> Paisley would make an amusing remark, which he did very well, and everyone would start laughing. And then he'd suddenly thump the table and say, 'What are you laughing at?

This is the fate of Ulster here, and you sit round the table laughing!' He was a bit of a magician.

The afternoon's work ranged over familiar ground: majority versus minority rights, the Government of Ireland Act, the Agreement, Sunningdale, the old Stormont, direct rule, and so on. Towards the end, a defensive Paisley agreed that he was suspicious of British governments just as much as of Irish ones, and that his loyalty was to the Queen, not to any specific government. By the day's end, very little useful engagement had been achieved, and even the points-scoring arguments had gone nowhere. But at least they were nearing the end of the tortuous and rhetoric-dominated phase of the questioning of the opening statements.

Friday morning began with Stephen convening a meeting of the six delegation leaders, to agree the details of adjourning for the summer and the initial steps for progress on resumption. Then in the plenary, the questioning of presentations finally ended, as the UUP defended its paper to the other delegations. There were more complaints about the continuing press leaks, but no resolution of the issue.

In the afternoon, the delegations tabled their written responses to the opening statements and the discussion of them. There was very little in any of the papers to inspire optimism. The Unionist papers addressed themselves almost entirely to lengthy critiques of the Irish opening statement, the DUP also providing a prolonged defence against nationalism in general. The Irish paper, another lengthy one from Wilson, was for the most part a recapitulation of their opening statement. The others tended to be polite expressions of optimism for more engaged discussion in September.

Then Stephen opened discussion of future arrangements. He presented a work plan for September, as drawn up by the Business Committee and approved at the earlier leaders' meeting. The plan was agreed. The Business Committee would reconvene on 1 September, and plenary on the following day. Parties were asked to table by 28 August their papers on Agenda Item 6: 'Fundamental Aspects of the Problem – Underlying Realities: Identity, Allegiance, Constitutional Issues.' The Business Committee would then consider these at its 1 September meeting, and recommend to the next day's plenary how best to go about the discussion of them. It was likely that they would recommend the formation of a sub-committee (with three delegates each) mandated to discuss the papers within a time limit and report back to plenary.

Although they would reconvene initially in Belfast, Stephen declared that 'the Strand 2 work programme will include a substantive meeting of Strand 2 in Dublin in September' (*Irish Times* 25 July 1992), with all that this would imply for Unionists in crossing the psychological barrier of negotiating on the Irish government's home turf. They had, of course, already crossed one symbolic rubicon by sitting in formal negotiation with the Irish delegation, and indeed the progress to date was of more symbolic than substantive importance. But doubts remained about the DUP, in particular, making that move. Paisley ended the day with a press statement in which he seemed to be keeping an exit strategy alive: 'Until the Irish government is prepared to ... give up its claim to the territory of Northern Ireland, then no real progress can be made' (*Irish Times* 25 July 1992). Over the weekend, he spelt out the strategy more clearly, complaining that the British had so far failed in their duty to confront the Irish over the territorial claim. The claim was, for Paisley, the make-or-break issue in the talks process. A referendum commitment was something 'we have to come to grips with, and will be coming to grips with finally – and I use the word "finally" – when we come back'. Otherwise, Dublin 'will be finishing the talks. We'll not be finishing the talks, they know that' (*Irish Times* 27 July 1992). Whatever his intention, his words were seen in Dublin as preparing the way for a DUP walk-out, at least for any meetings in the Republic. There were strongly negative views within his party on the value of the whole talks process, William McCrea having absented himself from anything to do with Strand 2 from the start because not enough Strand 1 progress had been made. Andrews heard the remarks 'more in sorrow than in anger' (*Irish Times* 29 July 1992). Seamus Close complained that Paisley was breaching the spirit of confidentiality with his remarks, and counselled against laying down such implausible preconditions (ibid.). By now, even the Australians were beginning to question the commitment and intent of the DUP. 'Who knows if Paisley was at all committed to the process?' mused Thompson:

He did sound surprisingly genuine and committed at our London meeting, and in one or two of the DUP papers. But the DUP quite often seemed to be schizophrenic, in some of the contributions, including those made by Paisley himself and by Robinson ... And then there was Denny Vitty for example: you'd have to say that he was only there as a spoiler.

To complete the important step of having all three strands opened before the recess, and thus facilitating progress in September, Mayhew and Hanley met with the full Irish government delegation (Wilson, Andrews, Flynn and O'Malley) in a formal Strand 3 meeting in Dublin's Iveagh House on Tuesday 28 July. They talked for four and a half hours, including a working lunch, reviewing all three strands to date, and setting the Strand 3 agenda for September. No comments were forthcoming from either side as they emerged through a knot of demonstrators demanding no change to the constitution, but they appeared upbeat, and the Irish delegation gave a 'highly positive report' to Reynolds at a subsequent Cabinet meeting (*Irish Times* 29 July 1992).

The formal sessions might have paused, but the leaks continued. The following day, Saturday, the full text of the Irish government's opening statement to Strand 2 was published in the *Irish Times*. Dublin was very angry, referring to Stephen's strong statement on the subject last week and declaring that talks would not make progress 'in an atmosphere of continuing leaks' (*Irish Times* 30 July 1992). But, angry or not, no one can have been too surprised at this latest breach. Publicly, all the participants had consistently emphasized the importance of confidentiality, but privately the media had had no shortage of eager informants.

And so the participants reached the respite of August. Apart from preparing the position papers for September, the priority in most minds at this stage was a holiday. Stephen and Thompson returned to Australia, pleased to have paused on a reasonably optimistic and positive note.

6
Resumption: 'Happiness Abounds': September

The politicians took their well-earned vacations during August. It was largely a quiet month, with some tension evident around seasonal marches in the North, and with Mayhew finally taking the long-threatened step of banning the loyalist paramilitary grouping, the UDA. On 27 August, Northern Ireland reached a depressing milestone as official RUC figures recorded the 3000th violent death of the Troubles.

The parties' papers on Item 6 (*Fundamental Aspects of the Problem: underlying realities; identity; allegiance; constitutional issues*) were duly submitted on 28 August, and promptly circulated. There was little of surprise in any of them. For the UUP, the *underlying realities* were statements of Unionist core principles, among them acknowledgement of Northern Ireland's status within the UK, Northern Ireland's right to self-determination, and its people's right to a democratically accountable system of government without exception or 'special arrangements'. On *identity*, the paper briefly repeated its Strand 2 opening statement on the need for mutual understanding, acknowledged that identity was central to nationalists, and pledged support for 'those accepted principles which deal with minority rights'. It addressed *allegiance* equally briefly, stating that: 'every citizen who rightly demands and achieves his [*sic*] place and role within a community has, first of all, an obligation and duty to that community. Ultimate affection, in aspirational terms, for either London or Dublin should not affect that basic truth.' Finally, under *constitutional* matters, the UUP declared their respect for the democratic process, and their distaste for the Anglo-Irish Agreement, and made some small suggestions for improving existing British–Irish structures, including an Irish and EC Affairs Committee within the new Strand 1 structure, and an Inter-Irish Relations Committee within Strand 2. There was no mention of the Irish constitution.

The DUP paper largely ignored the agenda headings, and began from the viewpoint that nothing could come of Strand 2 without a removal of Dublin's territorial claim on the North:

> It would be a positive starting-point for our deliberations if the government of the Irish Republic expressed a commitment to remove the territorial claim which offends us so deeply … In those circumstances, arrangements would be possible which we could not at present contemplate … No unionist can proceed any further without such a change.

There was little discussion of what the 'possible arrangements' alluded to might be, beyond improved relationships, the aim being 'that we might live as two countries on this island at peace and in friendship'. It was hardly likely to inspire any hope within nationalism.

The SDLP paper, like many others, was a revision of earlier papers, and frequently quoted the *New Ireland Forum Report* of 1984. Under the heading *'Underlying Realities, Identity and Allegiance'*, the paper stated that the problem was a conflict of identities, defined in exclusive terms, and a failure to devise political structures to accommodate them both; that partition had exacerbated the effect; and that recent changes, including the 1985 Anglo-Irish Agreement and the development of the EC, had improved the situation. It then listed the requirements of a new structure to address these realities, which included representing both identities so as to attract cross-community support in the North; broad all-Ireland scope; the capacity to promote harmony, co-operation and uniformity within the North and between North and South and to represent all interests in the EC; and the capacity to break down mistrust. The two sentences under *constitutional* aspects simply stated that such structures would have constitutional implications for all concerned.

The Alliance Party paper eschewed subheadings, and opened by reiterating its 'realities' from previous papers. Then it raised the need to remove the Irish claim to the North, offering to explore its own version of rewritten Articles at the appropriate time. Perhaps with an eye to DUP philosophy, it remarked that 'the existence of the Irish-Nationalist tradition requires that relations with the Republic of Ireland will consist of more than mere good neighbourliness'. And certainly in response to a familiar SDLP refrain was the assertion: 'the important task before us is not to agree an analysis, but to agree institutions which are capable of meeting our basic needs.' Finally, it recommended that the Strand 1 principles of workability, durability, stability and so on, should apply equally to Strand 2 structures.

The Irish government submitted two papers. The first, *Identity, Allegiance and Underlying Realities*, began with a long historical criticism of Unionism since the early 1900s. On the question of identities, it quoted from the 1984 *Forum Report* at great length. And, alluding to the Articles it offered a stiff bargain: 'If ... proposals for constitutional change emerging from the negotiations were to include changes to the Irish Constitution, the strength and quality of the proposed links between both parts of Ireland would be one of the important factors in shaping the judgement of the [Irish] electorate in this regard.' The second paper was titled *Constitutional Issues*. Claiming that constitutional change could not happen in only one direction, it set out a detailed nationalist case for amendment or removal of Britain's Government of Ireland Act (1920), which formed, 'in the unionist perspective, the legislative bedrock of Northern Ireland'. Then it defended in forthright manner the Irish constitution, which had 'been subject to severe and occasionally intemperate criticisms in the course of the Talks'. 'The Northern Ireland problem', the paper argued, 'existed before the Irish Constitution. The provisions of the Constitution reflect, rather than cause, the basic divisions.' It ended by not ruling out constitutional change on both sides, but reprising the need to offer the Irish electorate substantial gains in return.

The British government delegation paper was entitled *Fundamental Aspects, Common Interests and Themes, Other Requirements*. Regarding *realities*, an earlier Strand 1 paper was attached setting out some generalities about Northern Ireland not dissimilar to versions by any other party. On *identities and allegiances*, it briefly quoted from the Strand 1 Sub-Committee reports regarding the rights and necessities of giving expression to both identities. On *constitutional matters*, it simply quoted from Mayhew's opening statement to Strand 2 regarding the North's abiding status within the UK and the possible implications of that for Articles Two and Three. Then under the heading 'Common interests, themes and other requirements', it argued that an overall settlement needed the widespread allegiance and support in all parts of Ireland that would be engendered by including recognition of Northern Ireland's status in the UK while making provision for full expression of nationalist/Irish identity. It reviewed the general question of the potential for North–South co-operation on economic and trading matters. Finally, it set out a series of general principles regarding Strand 2 structures which might assist discussion (based on democratic principles, capable of delivering, acceptable, stable and durable, etc.).

With Wednesday 2 September set as the opening plenary, the Business Committee sat on Tuesday 1 to discuss the agenda. Their first agreement was to form a committee of four-person delegations to streamline the discussion of Agenda Item 6, and report to plenary on Thursday 10 September. But arranging the agenda for that committee proved difficult. The DUP wanted the Irish constitution at the top of the agenda; most of the other delegates disagreed. Dublin and the SDLP strongly objected, believing that any progress was now contingent on opening the Strand 2 debate out beyond this Unionist focus on the Irish constitution. While Dublin were happy to repeat their familiar mantra that 'everything was on the table for discussion', they were resolutely opposed to playing such a high card outside of a comprehensive settlement package. In the end, the meeting broke up with little agreement and a great deal of antagonism.

Wednesday's plenary was 'calm and reasonable' (*Irish Times* 3 September 1992). They agreed to form the 'Strand 2 Committee', and gave the four-delegate teams considerable negotiating powers, agreeing that it would meet the following day and on Tuesday and Wednesday of the next week before reporting to a plenary on Thursday. Hopes that this committee might be more streamlined than the ungainly plenary were dashed when the Irish delegation upped the ante by nominating their four government ministers to the Strand 2 Committee. All the others (with the exception of the British) responded by nominating their leaders and three senior members. Thompson recalls the resulting confusion:

> When we moved to the committee stage, what we found was that
> the committee was basically the plenary under another guise.
> Everyone wanted their full team, and for the most part the faces
> at the table were the same. So we were in this rather unusual
> position of resolving ourselves into committee, and then
> resolving ourselves into plenary to take the report of the
> committee back into plenary, and seek the guidance of the
> plenary for further work in committee!

Formal agreement was also secured for moving the talks to Dublin
later in the month, and Stephen asked for nominees from each delegation to liaise over the arrangements for this. However, the DUP
were holding their position on Articles Two and Three as strongly
as ever, with the implication that without a referendum commitment a Dublin meeting would be pointless.

The new Strand 2 Committee met that afternoon, and managed
some agreement on small procedural matters. But the rest of the
meeting slipped into an accusatory session, featuring in particular
the DUP and the Irish delegation. They were trying to agree on a
detailed agenda for all issues relevant to Item 6, but the DUP's
relentless pursuit of Articles Two and Three, and Dublin's equally
relentless defence of them, were blocking progress.

They met again the next morning, Thursday. Stephen suggested
they begin by each outlining what they saw as the obstacles in the way
of building new North–South relationships; his hope was that out of
those obstacles would arise the ingredients of an agenda. Ken
Maginnis objected that this was too negative a way to begin, and
would lead to confrontation. The Alliance's Seamus Close agreed that
it would lead to a repeat of yesterday's session of 'wallowing around'.
Hume suggested they list both obstacles and positive aspects. Flynn
agreed that a list of obstacles would be a good start; Hanley concurred.
Paisley complained that every time he mentioned an obstacle, all the
other delegations complained that he was raising preconditions, and
went on to say that the Union might be seen by some as an obstacle,
but it was absolutely non-negotiable. Eventually, they adjourned for
45 minutes to permit each delegation to produce their list of obstacles
on blank paper without any indication of the source.

On their return, they each read their list. They were predictably accusatory and confrontational lists, ranging from three items to ten. Then Stephen offered a composite list of seven headings. Andrews objected that the Government of Ireland Act was too far down the list, given Dublin's view of its importance. Paisley jumped in to assert that the Act, the basis of Northern Ireland's constitutional status, was not up for discussion. He threatened to leave if there was any talk about negotiating the Union, and demanded an adjournment to consult with the rest of his delegation. It was granted after a few minutes' delay, but on return he took immediate issue with Stephen for not granting an automatic and immediate adjournment on request from a party leader, as specified in the standing orders for Strand 2.

Eventually, Stephen produced a redrafted list, putting the most frequently mentioned items at the top. Andrews again objected that Articles Two and Three were at the top of the list, while the Government of Ireland Act was relegated to the third paragraph. This led to a long detour concerning methods of making lists without implying prioritization, the value of unnumbered lists, the possibility of giving each item its own sheet of paper, etc. Hume called for a note of realism to acknowledge that the argument was couched among everyone's fears of documents being leaked. Mallon complained that there was far too much paper involved in the talks. Hume eventually called for the formal withdrawal of Stephen's draft, seconded by Andrews. Amidst mounting confusion, Hanley came to Stephen's rescue, suggesting they give the Chair fifteen minutes to redraft the list. Thompson recalls the moment wryly:

> We just very quickly got into an impossible situation around the table. All the delegations were there, no one knew where to take it, and almost to a man [sic] they just looked at Sir Ninian and said, 'Well, okay, you've got ten minutes, go and sort this one out.' So we went out to the next room and looked at each other and thought, 'What is this? Has it ground to a halt so quickly? And why is it that no one seems to have an idea of where to take it at this point?' Anyhow, we had literally ten or fifteen minutes to find a way through the impasse, so we came up with a proposal about a logical structure to the agenda.

Their proposed final version had four sub-items:

1. North–South channels of co-operation and communication
2. Terrorism and lack of co-operation on security
3. Identity and allegiance of the nationalist community
4. Constitutional matters.

Paisley rejected it, and said that if it was adopted, then the DUP would simply emulate the SDLP in Strand 1, by reserving their position on everything, until Articles Two and Three were reached in discussion of sub-item 4. 'There is a nettle which needs to be grasped, and we need to grasp it!' he declared. Thompson admits that 'This was probably the first moment in the talks when we fully realised the strength of feeling behind the position that the DUP were taking.'

Flynn proposed that sub-item 2 be phrased more positively (i.e., 'terrorism and co-operation on security'), to heated objections from Paisley and Robinson. It was amended to 'Lack of adequate channels of communication and co-operation between North and South'. Eventually, Stephen could see no possibility of consensus, and reluctantly asked for a vote: the amended list was accepted by all but the DUP. It was clear that not only were Dublin and the SDLP getting tired of accommodating DUP sensibilities, but even the UUP were now openly embarrassed by Paisley's posturing, and were trying to distance themselves from their Unionist partners. When it proved possible, there were constructive exchanges between the UUP and the Irish delegation, but everyone was growing increasingly annoyed with the DUP derailing discussions.

Later that same day, an SDLP grouping met with Reynolds and the Irish government team. The Dublin delegation told their allies that it was their considered opinion that Mayhew would not accept the SDLP Strand 1 proposal as long as it included the executive Panel concept. Mayhew, they said, had declared the Panel totally unsaleable to Unionists. Their belief was that the talks would therefore break down by the end of the month, as it became clear that the Conference meeting could not be postponed for much longer. The meeting consequently began to make contingency plans for how best to position the SDLP prior to the breakdown.

On the next negotiating day, Wednesday 9 September, the Strand

2 Committee resumed deliberations. While others wanted to move on to substantive discussions on the agenda as agreed, the DUP resumed their demand that sub-item 4 be moved to the top of the agenda so that they could begin with Articles Two and Three. They passed a statement to Stephen for circulation, advising that without such alteration they would reserve their position on every agenda item. When the demand was denied, Paisley walked out at midday, quickly followed by Robinson. Their remaining two delegates, Sammy Wilson and Gregory Campbell, became 'observers' to the talks, and the party declared that they would not return to the table officially until the agenda had been worked through as far as sub-item 4. The UUP also passed around a statement, expressing their own disapproval of the ordering of the agenda but announcing that they would remain at the table 'under the principle "Nothing is agreed until everything is agreed"'.

With the DUP reduced to observers, the committee began work on Agenda sub-item 1 after lunch. To the facilitators' eyes, it proved the most positive day of negotiation so far: a view clearly tied to the DUP's absence. A British paper on possible North–South institutions was tabled and discussed until 9pm that evening. But the paper contained a short fuse that ignited further fireworks. Under a variety of headings, it offered broad ranges of options for consideration, including one of setting up a Southern government office in Belfast and a Northern office in Dublin, and other options concerning the degree of 'executive power' which might be vested in the institutions. Moreover, although written by a member of the British delegation, the paper contained instances of 'Humespeak' (such as 'an agreed Ireland', and a proposed North–South commission with 'its own powers of initiative on the EC model') guaranteed to anger Unionists simply by its recognizable authorship. The suggestion implicit in some parts of the paper – which in its defence was merely a wide review of differing options offered to aid discussion – appeared to a Unionist eye to hint at nascent joint authority. UUP delegates were content to continue with discussions of the paper, despite their opposition to its content. But Molyneaux, who had not participated in the day's sessions, was incensed that evening when he saw it, and directed considerable fury at the NIO. More strategically, the paper was unlikely to have any effect on the UUP leadership other than to threaten them and thus move their position closer to the DUP line of demanding prior commitment from Dublin on Articles Two and Three before agreeing anything else on the Strand 2 agenda.

The evening's row continued into Thursday's meeting of the Committee. Despite the DUP's 'semi-detached' involvement as observers only, enough UUP delegates had caught their leader's mood to make it a difficult day. They presented a brief UUP statement announcing their overall objection to the British paper and their specific rejection of 11 particular paragraphs of it. A very brief plenary meeting was held as scheduled at the end of the day to agree three more negotiating days the following week. The DUP completely boycotted the meeting. They did, however, offer a written statement to the plenary:

> The Ulster Democratic Unionist Party [sic] want to make it perfectly clear that we reserve our position as far as all the proceedings of this committee are concerned since our negotiators left the table, and we dispute the accuracy of the outline given in the report of events in the committee. We disassociate ourselves from HMG's [sic] paper of [yesterday ...] and protest against the attempt in that paper to direct talks towards an 'Agreed Ireland'. We wish to put on record that as far as the UDUP are concerned, many parts of HMG's paper are a clear surrender of the Unionist majority's position and are intolerable. Thus far, [sub-item] 1 has not been realistically dealt with.

In contrast to the DUP's view, however, the other parties did manage enough progress on sub-item 1 to agree a set of principles to underpin co-operation and communication between North and South, which were closely based on those principles (durability, stability, etc.) agreed for a Strand 1 formula.

On Friday 11 September, British and Irish ministers held a Strand 3 meeting in London. But the meeting was overshadowed by the growing Unionist anger. The controversial British Strand 2 paper was leaked the same day, and appeared in Saturday's press. Molyneaux responded by telling the *Irish Times* just how far his line had hardened:

> If it becomes clear in a few weeks' time that the Irish government

has no intention of removing its illegal claim to Northern Ireland, then we cannot and we will not continue with our discussions – they will have given a clear signal that the shutters have come down. (*Irish Times* 14 September 1992)

His UUP delegates remained more sanguine, and the SDLP entirely silent, on the matter, while the NIO claimed the document was merely to stimulate discussion. But a DUP source remained sceptical of that, and expressed suspicion of the British agenda: 'Well, I don't accept it was just to encourage discussion. I don't accept that any participant would put into their own document suggestions that were alien to them' (*Irish Times* 14 September 1992).

In the hope, no doubt, of enraging the Unionist public, the Irish opening statement to Strand 2 was leaked on Tuesday 15. It became clear to all that Dublin's price for amending their constitution was substantial North–South institutionalization. Among the delegates, it was common knowledge that Dublin wished for a North–South entity, or range of entities, with a degree of executive power. That such 'executive power' was specifically mentioned in the *British* paper was bound to provoke Unionist anger inside Stormont. For their part, the DUP called the published Irish position 'obnoxious, immoral, illegal and criminal' (*Irish Times* 16 September 1992).

As the Strand 2 Committee resumed its deliberations on Wednesday 16 September, the DUP, still observing in 'semi-detached' manner, appeared to be upping the ante. Despite brisk work by the Committee which meant that they were already on to sub-item 3 of the agenda, *Identities and Allegiances in Northern Ireland* (i.e., the one before Constitutional matters), the DUP were now demanding not only that the Articles be discussed, but that there be evidence of them being 'realistically addressed' before there could be any DUP trips to Dublin (*Irish Times* 17 September 1992). Paisley joined the other delegations for a plenary briefing on the previous week's Strand 3 meeting, but left again immediately afterwards. The obstinacy and inflexibility of the DUP position was becoming increasingly aggravating to everyone, and Stephen and Thompson were beginning to rethink their objectives, as Thompson elaborates:

Just before we went to Dublin, it became fairly apparent at least to Sir Ninian and me that it was going to be impossible to produce an agreement that the DUP would be part of. That whatever concessions you might be able to wring from the Irish in particular, they wouldn't be sufficient to get the DUP on board. So we came to the conclusion early on that that was going to be too much to hope for.

Specifically, the continuing DUP series of preconditions were increasingly treated not as serious substantive points, but merely as obstructive tactics to hold up the process:

First of all, we thought they would never get the first precondition they were looking for, the further progress [on Strand 1]. And we were never really convinced that if they did get that precondition they would then talk turkey on the other blockages – like unambiguous recognition of the constitutional status of Northern Ireland, the executive authority for a North–South institution, and so on. They used to say, and in writing, that if the Irish were prepared to make that concession, then their attitude would change entirely. But nobody believed that! (Thompson)

The Committee finished sub-item 3 by close of business on Thursday, which left the discussion of constitutional matters the first order of business for Friday. Paisley and Robinson led their full team back to the table on Friday, and each delegation outlined their views on the subject in a paper. The DUP continued their pattern of reserving their position, and once more insisted on a statement to that effect being annexed to the day's minutes. Once again an argument developed, this time between the two Unionist parties over the circumstances in which it had been agreed to move Strand 2 to Dublin. Andrews told the Committee of his government's willingness to accept constitutional change provided that the negotiations as a whole 'achieved the basis of a new beginning in the relationship between the two traditions in Ireland' (*Irish Times* 21 September 1992). The UUP accepted that as a softening of the position. But it cut no ice with the DUP. That evening, Paisley told reporters that his party would not even send observers to next week's Dublin meetings. The UUP were annoyed at the boycott, but the SDLP, Dublin and even the Australian facilitators suspected the entire argument had been manufactured to permit Paisley to avoid travelling to Dublin. Stephen admits that his own optimism on the question got the better of him: 'I thought he might go to Dublin. It seemed so pointless not to, such an empty gesture. But he knows his congregation better than I do, and perhaps it would have seemed to be a retreat. I think internal reasons within his own party had a lot to do with it. Thompson recounts how the suspicion grew:

> The silly procedural manoeuvrings that we got into in the lead-up to Dublin proved that beyond doubt the DUP were looking for an excuse not to go to Dublin. We tried desperately not to give them that excuse. In the end, their excuse was that we would not accede to their demand that there be just a plenary meeting in Dublin. We regarded Dublin as a continuing part of the whole process, and it wasn't simply to have a single plenary meeting. Sir Ninian wasn't prepared to budge on that.

Over the weekend, DUP sources admitted that they might well return to the talks in the following week, when they resumed at Stormont. Chris McGimpsey, a UUP moderate, told BBC Radio Ulster that the Irish government needed to get specific on the Articles during next week's talks in Dublin, and complained that so far they had remained too vague: 'We've seen nothing specific at all. It's all philosophical debate and so on – we all love one another, and we're all going to deal with this problem – but we haven't got around to deciding what the problem is yet' (*Irish Times* 21 September 1992).

When several Sunday newspapers carried reports of Andrews' words in Friday's Committee meeting, Maginnis told RTE that he recognized a softer line in the remarks:

> If this was the Irish government's attitude, then I think we would be on the way to meeting the hopes of my party's delegation in so far as we would like an agreement in principle that certain things can happen in relation to Articles Two and Three, and yet that we understand the implementation of those measures need not happen until other issues have been agreed. (*Irish Times* 21 September 1992)

A Dublin source claimed Andrews had simply been restating the consistent position of the Irish government from the start. Robinson saw nothing new to interest him in the remarks, while McCrea declared the UUP's trip to Dublin next Monday 'a betrayal of the loyalist people' (*Irish Times* 21 September 1992).

On the eve of the historic arrival of Unionist negotiators in Dublin, a row emerged within the Irish cabinet. While Reynolds had been in the US during the week, it had become apparent that both the Progressive Democrat (PD) cabinet ministers, O'Malley and Molloy, would be unavailable for some of the week's sessions. Andrews had approved the PD junior Environment minister, Mary Harney, as a replacement. But on his return on Sunday morning, Reynolds vetoed her involvement, despite her party leader O'Malley's protestations. While Reynolds argued that only senior cabinet ministers should be involved, it looked very much as if he was unwilling to allow any more PDs into the delegation, given the differences of opinion on Articles Two and Three that had already surfaced between his own Fianna Fail party and the PDs.

On the morning of Monday 21 September, Molyneaux led an unsmiling UUP delegation into Dublin Castle. An unofficial version insists that he made sure to have a briefcase in each hand as he walked in, so as to avoid any possibility of a public handshake with the Irish government delegation waiting outside the door. Whatever the accuracy of such a story, it certainly symbolized the attitude of the UUP leader. 'If we're talking about commitment to the process,' remarks Thompson, 'we always suspected that Molyneaux had made a political judgement early on that the process wasn't going to lead anywhere. And that his reputation wasn't going to be tainted as a consequence ... He was always distant and uncommitted.'

The plenary convened and approved the Strand 2 Committee's progress report, which delineated some small progress over sub-items 2 and 3, and asked plenary to extend its remit to cover Items 7–9 of the Agenda and make a final report to plenary on Wednesday. (*Item 7: Common interests, including matters such as economic co-operation, employment, security co-operation and law enforcement; Item 8: Other requirements to address the problem; Item 9: Possible institutional arrangements to meet the requirements, including principles to govern any successful arrangements*). The request was granted. Despite objections from several parties, Stephen acceded to a DUP request that, despite their absence, a statement from them be annexed to the meeting's minutes. The statement was predictably critical of the discussions:

> The UDUP [*sic*] continues to reserve its position as far as all the proceedings of this committee are concerned since its negotiators withdrew from the table. The UDUP note that consideration of these fundamental issues has not led to any criticism of the deplorable security policies presently employed nor the adoption of any principles placing a duty upon delegations to encourage support of the Crown services in Northern Ireland ... We further note that the committee's interpretation of Agenda Item 6 was to dilute it to a consideration of possible principles rather than substantive negotiation.

Following the plenary, the Committee went into session for a full day. With the DUP absent, the debate become noticeably more substantive. The British tabled another paper on possible structures for North–South co-operation, this time a more anodyne version than the previous paper which had generated such anger from Molyneaux. But once again, the discussion gradually returned to focus on the question of the Irish constitution, and forthright talking between the Irish and UUP delegations both exposed the bedrock positions on both sides and made for heated arguments. Little progress was made, beyond the clear delineation of those positions.

Undoubtedly, for the Irish government, the main coup of the day was the symbolism of having Unionist negotiators present and engaged for the first time in Dublin. Emerging at 5.15pm, Andrews declared 'Happiness abounds at Dublin Castle!' (*Irish Times* 22 September 1992), although the tensions within his own delegation and the tight-lipped Unionist demeanour might have argued otherwise. A little later, from his own side of the border, Paisley voiced to BBC television his colourful criticism of the UUP for fraternizing with the enemy in Dublin, revisiting the ground-rules he had laid out for Stephen at their first meeting:

> Some of the Unionist negotiators drink at the bar with these men

[the Irish delegation], they sit at the table with them, they wine and dine with them, and are on a Christian-name calling [basis]. My party is not in that business. We don't socialise with them. The only time we address them is across a table, when we are standing up for what Ulster stands for! (*Irish Times* 22 September 1992)

Critics might have added that addressing the Irish government was reserved for certain tables only, and none of them south of the border. Paisley asserted further that he was sure the discussions would not reach Articles Two and Three before the end of the Dublin round, and that he'd be back at the Northern table soon enough when the agenda reached that sub-item.

In contrast to Paisley's prediction, and undoubtedly to his disgust, on Tuesday the Committee focused for the day on that very issue. The UUP demanded that Dublin give at least a principled commitment to promote a referendum to change its constitution. In return, Dublin offered only a statement that it *could* promote such a referendum. The UUP insisted on a statement that they *would* do so. As the day went on, the immovability of both sides brought the talks close to collapse. Eventually, it was the UUP who blinked, and accepted the Dublin assurance with the greatest reluctance, on the understanding that the subject would be revisited later. From the Irish point of view, however, offering such an assurance, even only in principle, was a substantial concession. Thompson recognized it as such, and was encouraged:

We were probably at our most pessimistic just prior to the Dublin meeting. But the Dublin session was a good one. Real progress was made ... We felt – and I think a lot of the parties felt – that there were some important breakthroughs. That was where the Irish agreed to the formulation, as part of an overall compromise or settlement, that they could sponsor a referendum to change Articles Two and Three. We had a lot of arguing over substituting *would* for *could*. But nevertheless the UUP agreed that that was progress, and sufficient basis on which to keep talking.

Publicly, UUP negotiators simply described the day as 'constructive and business-like', adding that they detected no softening of the Irish position on the matter. Stephen and his wife went off to lunch with Irish President Mary Robinson, while Maginnis, Empey, the McGimpseys and some of the other Ulster Unionists escaped the press and chose a Dublin pub for a quiet lunch. Their party leader had attended briefly in the morning before leaving for Westminster.

In the evening, the two government delegations met for a Strand 3 session, where the main item for discussion was the impending Conference meeting. The Irish expressed strong reluctance to postpone the Conference meeting further (and, therefore, the end of talks) beyond the end of October. Mayhew only managed to dissuade them by appealing over their heads to Reynolds and Major to consider a later deadline. That evening, the Taoiseach and Prime Minister spoke by phone and agreed to discuss the Conference date further when they would meet on EC business in London at the end of the week. It was now the British goal to aim for a more minimal Heads of Agreement document by the close of talks. While Wilson told the press the meeting had been 'very fruitful', and Mayhew declared that the talks were 'coming right' (*Irish Times* 23 September 1992), no one else was making any comment.

On Wednesday, the Committee moved on to matters of North–South economic and security co-operation. It was a quieter day, with Dublin and the UUP finding more common ground on these issues, and Stephen was able to steer the discussion gently on to more fruitful ground. Both sides spent the day constructively, sending, receiving and acknowledging signals from each other. Once again, despite their absence, the DUP managed to have inserted in the meeting's minutes a protest note claiming their inability to discuss any other items until 'progress has been made on the key and central issue'. There was no plenary that day, it being agreed to permit the Committee to continue its work for a longer period.

As the Dublin round ended, the UUP released a statement declaring that they were happy to have fulfilled their obligation to talk in Dublin: 'We are well prepared to argue the Ulster Unionist case whenever and wherever we are given the opportunity' (*Irish Times* 24 September 1992). There had been little substantive progress in the week, but the historic significance of a Unionist delegation entering Dublin Castle had been no small achievement.

That evening, Reynolds commented on the urgency of the looming deadline: 'I know the talks are important, but so is the Conference and I do not want its importance to be devalued' (*Irish Times* 24 September 1992).

He continued the theme in his meeting with John Major on Friday. He argued that with five months gone since the last Conference meeting, they were beginning to risk weakening the Agreement's structures to please the Unionists. The Conference needed to meet within a month. On the other hand, Major and Mayhew countered, it was vital that the talks continue: it was clear that at the present pace they would need a lot more time, and that this was reason enough to override Conference arrangements for a month or two. In the end, they compromised: the Conference meeting would take place on 16 November, a 'firm and immutable' date, according to Reynolds, with 'no further extensions', according to Major (*Irish Times* 26 September 1992). In turn, the UUP Executive Council met in Belfast and declared themselves happy that the postponement until November would permit enough time to reach agreement (ibid.). No doubt, they were delighted at any postponement of Conference meetings, which had always been an Irish concession to Unionists, largely symbolic in its importance of 'suspending' the Agreement. Whatever the reason, there were now at most six weeks left for talks.

Reynolds addressed a Fianna Fail dinner that evening, reassuring his party faithful that 'Articles Two and Three of the Constitution are not for sale, and you can be certain of this' (*Irish Times* 28 September 1992). Maginnis complained bitterly of the 'inflexible and aggressive stance of the Taoiseach' (ibid.), and Molloy of the PDs criticized the overly unaccommodating remark (*Irish Times* 13 November 1992). The Fianna Fail–Progressive Democrat argument rumbled on, to Unionist delight.

Meanwhile, in a move that would have outraged most, and utterly dumbfounded all, other participants, Mayhew sent a message through the confidential channel to Sinn Fein which reported the lack of progress in the talks. 'We were,' claimed Sinn Fein, 'being given consistent reports from the British government representative that the Brooke/Mayhew talks were going nowhere and that the government's prediction was that they would end in failure. We were also being told that there was friction between the senior civil servants (in London and Stormont) and Mayhew' (Sinn Fein, 1993, p. 13). It seemed that Mayhew was speaking in a far more forthright and pessimistic manner to the Republicans than he had at the negotiation table, where he had largely maintained his habitual air of genial bonhomie.

7
'Yes! We're Going to Crack This!': September–November

When the Business Committee reconvened at Stormont on the last Monday of September to agree the agenda for Strand 2 talks on Wednesday, Thursday and Friday, they decided that the first item for the week would be 'Item 9: Possible institutional arrangements to meet the requirements, including the principles to govern any such arrangements'. Despite DUP pressure, they rejected a proposal to widen the definition of Item 9 so that it could include more discussion of Articles Two and Three. The DUP reaction was to announce the following day that their boycott would continue. Sammy Wilson told the press, 'We would be there if they were discussing Articles Two and Three, but they are quite clearly not' (*Irish Times* 30 September 1992).

But by Wednesday morning, the DUP had decided that Item 9 did in fact fulfil their need to discuss the Articles, and they turned up for the Strand 2 Committee. Indeed, the DUP immediately began to claim they had won a concession on the agenda, an opinion that deeply irritated all other participants, who 'heaped scorn upon' the DUP's continuing histrionics (*Irish Times* 1 October 1992).

Stephen started the day by setting the priority of addressing Agenda Item 9, the better to return subsequently to the core issue of constitutional change under Item 6, sub-item 4. Although most participants had unofficially accepted that the general discussions of the Strand 2 talks were now over, and it was time to start proper negotiations, the DUP continued their tactic of introducing procedural disputes once again to side-track any potential negotiations into arguments. Robinson returned to the accusation that the SDLP had tabled a devolution proposal to Strand 1 in June which they knew in advance was both unacceptable and incapable of winning the necessary widespread cross-community support. Therefore, he concluded, the SDLP never had any serious intent of negotiating in Strand 1. It was the kind of argument almost guaranteed to distract at least the Northern participants from the task in hand, even as the Irish government delegation tabled its own paper on North–South institutions. The Irish, for their part, also tabled a statement on constitutional change, essentially expressing their frustration that negotiations could be stalled by the DUP over this one element, and insisting that the banking principle should free Unionists to discuss that and every other issue without prejudice to their ultimate position. But it was less than well received by the DUP.

The talking eventually moved on to address the Irish paper on North–South institutional arrangements. In an attempt to continue his 'gentle steering' of the previous negotiating day, Stephen identified two matching reluctances around the table: one to accept the *de facto* position of Northern Ireland within the UK, and one to accept any North–South institutions in case they proved to be precursors for a united Ireland. At the same time, he noted, both governments had agreed to the principle of no change to the North's status without the consent of its population. Such a principle ought to reassure Unionists that there could be no moves towards Irish unity without their consent, while encouraging nationalists to hope for unity through evolution and persuasion. If that principle was accepted, he argued, they ought to be able to put aside much of the conflict of the past week and engage more positively.

But Maginnis drew the focus of the day back once again to the Irish constitution, launching a heavy attack on Reynolds's statement of the previous week that Articles Two and Three 'were not for sale'. Tempers rose, and Stephen called an emergency coffee-break. Having consulted with both the government delegations, he reconvened the meeting and tried to calm fears by recalling the banking principle: if it was accepted that 'nothing is agreed until everything is agreed', there should be no reason for any party to doubt that a full, three-stranded agreement would include Irish constitutional change as part of full implementation. With that intervention, he turned the debate back to the Irish paper on North–South institutions. But on this item, too, Dublin and the UUP quickly became deadlocked, as Padraig Flynn in particular took a provocatively hard-line position.

Discussion of the paper continued throughout Thursday 1 October. Robinson used the discussion cleverly to rehearse yet again some fundamental DUP beliefs about the constitutional position of Northern Ireland; in return the Irish delegation gave an unconvincing performance. While their paper remained largely at the level of general principle, it did contain some sections which were bound to provoke Unionist disagreement: new structures should have 'explicit institutional status and capacity ... a clear measure of institutional autonomy ... and an expressly executive function'. All of these were much more substantial than Unionists would want, since their aim was to retain as much power as possible in the Strand 1 structures, and consequently as little as possible in the Strand 2 ones. The Business Committee sat briefly on Thursday, to consider a work schedule proposed by Stephen: for the rest of the week the Committee would concentrate on Agenda Item 9, and the following week's sessions (Wednesday to Friday) would involve drawing up a progress report on Committee discussions of Items 6–9 for that Friday afternoon's plenary. The plan was agreed, and Stephen ended the meeting with a gentle reminder to the parties that they should be considering an appropriate time to resume Strand 1 talks.

On Friday the British and the Northern parties tabled their own papers on institutional arrangements, and then the Irish delegation faced cross-examination on theirs. At this rate, as they ended the first of the remaining six weeks, there was no hope of any conclusion by mid-November.

On the following Wednesday and Thursday, 7 and 8 October, sessions of the Strand 2 Committee were taken up with efforts to draft the progress report for Friday's plenary. Irish ministers were absent, attending the official opening of the Dail, while British ministers were in England for the Conservative Party conference, and so a Strand 3 meeting scheduled for Thursday was cancelled. On the Wednesday, a drafting group, of two members per delegation, worked on a draft report to plenary drawn up by Stephen. They presented this to the Strand 2 Committee on Thursday, but the Committee could not agree over Articles Two and Three. The draft read, in part:

The Alliance, UDUP, UK government and UUP delegations pressed for a commitment from the Irish government to sponsor an amendment to Articles Two and Three ... The Irish government delegation pointed to the importance of such factors as the satisfactory expression of nationalist aspirations and the strength and quality of the links between both parts of Ireland in shaping the judgement of the electorate on such an issue. If agreement were to be reached in the current talks on a fair and honourable accommodation between the two traditions in Ireland, the Irish government could approach its electorate with the hope and prospect of a positive response ... It was agreed that this issue remained open.

The description of the Irish position was far too conditional for UUP and Alliance tastes, and the DUP demanded that its own hard-line rejection of the position be included in the wording of the report:

The UDUP stated that it saw the key and central issue to be addressed as being the Republic of Ireland's 'territorial claim' to Northern Ireland. The UDUP indicated they could not consider or negotiate on common interests (Item 7), other requirements (Item 8) or possible institutional arrangements (Item 9) until progress had been made on 'the key and central issue'.

The SDLP and UUP offered their own alternatives to the DUP. The UUP 'would require the Government of the Irish Republic now to accept, in principle, the need to sponsor changes in the Constitution, including the necessary referendum, to address their fears and concerns.' The SDLP tried to couch consent in an all-Ireland context. Finally, the UUP softened its version by adding the phrase, 'subject to a satisfactory conclusion of the talks as a whole'. But no compromise was found between the competing versions, and no agreed draft was reached. In the eyes of the Australian facilitators, it was increasingly clear by this stage that the DUP were no longer engaged in any substantive negotiation process, but were working simply to wreck the talks. While their refusal to discuss anything but Articles Two and Three was making their contribution to the debate 'mercifully minimal', it was the Australian view that they had successfully steered the fairly productive discussion on North–South structures back onto the rocks of the constitutional issue. In response to such Unionist intransigence, the Dublin delegation seemed to be disillusioned with the entire talks process, and more than ready to match any intransigence with their own. Any Irish hopes of agreement, it seemed to the facilitators, had completely vanished by this point. For their part, the British appeared exasperated with both the Unionists and the Irish delegation, and resigned to the impending end of the talks process, although still nursing faint hopes of some breakthrough before then which would enable a prompt restart.

By Friday morning, 9 October, another argument had erupted over the progress report. Essentially, the DUP insisted that there was no progress to report, and there would be none until Dublin gave a firm commitment to hold a referendum on the Articles, while the UUP claimed to discern a hint of a softening Irish approach on the matter. The SDLP angrily accused the DUP of defining progress as only whatever 'fell in 100 per cent with their demands' (*Irish Times* 10 October 1992). The DUP reserved their position on every item under discussion, insisting they could not give opinions on any of the topics until a prior commitment to constitutional change was forthcoming from Dublin. The progress report was shelved, the plenary cancelled, and Stephen merely asked permission to continue Committee discussions for a further week.

For the rest of the day, the talks focused on discussion of the DUP and UUP papers. But the DUP admitted that their own paper was short of concrete proposals on North–South institutions, since they were not prepared to offer serious proposals until the referendum commitment was given by Dublin. The British delegation, meanwhile, tabled a lengthy paper on Item 9. It was an attempt to summarize the debate to date, but consisted mainly of a statement of very general principles which were largely agreed for North–South structures, and a long list of questions over which there had been very little agreement, in particular the question of the degree of executive authority to be vested in the structures. It was an accurate snapshot of the state of play in the Committee, but it was highly unlikely to inspire any breakthroughs.

Stephen ended the day by canvassing opinion on procedural changes to the process which might encourage movement. In particular, he had in mind a process where the UUP and SDLP might agree on some kind of package, for which the SDLP could then gain Irish support while the UUP elicited at least acquiescence from Paisley's party. But even he, privately, accepted that they were now going round in ever-decreasing circles and that a breakthrough looked very remote.

UUP frustration at their Unionist partners, and strategic attempts to undermine Dublin's refusal to concede on the Articles, led the party to leak its own position paper on Friday evening. Saturday's *Irish Times* carried details of their proposals. Although the DUP called them 'absolute idiots' for playing their cards face up (*Irish Times* 12 October 1992) there was little drama in the UUP paper. It proposed 'good neighbourliness' between the two parts of Ireland, but contained no trace of cross-border institutions with any degree of power. Dublin and the SDLP gave cautious and uninformative public reactions.

Although in general participants began to speak of a phase of getting down to specific business after the preceding weeks of general rhetoric, the DUP seemed impervious to such ideas. They announced on Monday 12 October that they would withdraw from the talks a week before the Conference meeting, effectively cutting the time left to four weeks. Their complaints about Dublin and accusations towards the UUP mounted in intensity. Having laughed the leaked UUP proposals out of court two days earlier, Sammy Wilson declared, in relation to the 4-week time-limit they had imposed, 'We will not pull back from doing what is necessary to blow the whistle on the betrayal being concocted with Unionist connivance behind closed doors at Stormont' (*Irish Times* 13 October 1992).

On Tuesday, Paisley went further. He rejected the British suggestion adopted by Reynolds and Major that perhaps a more reasonable goal for the remaining time would be a skeleton Heads of Agreement document. He insisted that he would not sign even that without the referendum commitment from Dublin. Mayhew continued to talk the idea up in optimistic fashion, but the DUP were by now very effectively stalling and diverting the talks process, and frustration was growing in the other parties. 'We're not locked in to an engaging debate on political issues,' one delegate complained to the *Irish Times*. 'There's a lot of arguing over procedural issues and a lot of posturing. We see glimpses of debate over fundamental issues, but then they're gone again' (*Irish Times* 14 October 1992). Lost amid the posturing and the procedures, the progress report scheduled for the previous Friday's plenary had now been abandoned altogether.

Nevertheless, the delegations all arrived at Stormont on Wednesday morning for the first of the week's three Strand 2 Committee days. Before the start of business, Mayhew met quietly with the Irish delegation. He put to them a dramatic idea for raising the stakes of the talks. With only a few weeks left, he suggested that they accelerate the process by opening it out to all three Strands and working towards the creation of a comprehensive Heads of Agreement document. Thus while broadening the scope of the talks, he hoped to reduce the depth of agreement needed to produce what could be called a positive result. He acknowledged the risk involved, but suggested that Stephen had the necessary flair and sensitivity for his role that might make it possible for him to carry it off. The Irish, already deep in pessimism, agreed that it was worth the effort.

The Committee was convened and, still with Item 9, they spent some time hearing the SDLP elaborating on their idea of a Council of Ministers. But Stephen himself was conscious that the debate had reached stagnation. Now was the time to either inject new life, or call a halt to the whole process. 'We had all reached the stage by 14 October where everyone agreed that we were going nowhere in the format we had been following,' Thompson recalled:

> The Irish government, more so than the British, were not prepared to keep extending the gap between meetings of the Anglo-Irish Conference ... So we knew we only had a few weeks left, and if we kept going in the current format we wouldn't get anywhere. So Sir Ninian came up with a couple of options.

Over lunch, Mayhew took his suggestion to Stephen, who readily agreed to put the idea to the Committee in the afternoon session. Reconvening the meeting, he offered them the options of continuing to discuss Item 9 in the hope of reaching some convergence on North–South structures, or of radically expanding the agenda laterally to embrace all three Strands, but to set their sights on the lower goal of a Heads of Agreement document which would sketch, in Stephen's words, the 'elements of a settlement'. After discussion, they chose the second option. Stephen was very pleased, agreeing that: 'It seems to me to offer the best prospect of achieving a break-through in the time remaining.' But he also warned that it was a high-risk strategy to thus up the ante:

> If we are unable to agree on the broad content a new agreement might take, there can be little prospect of making further progress in these talks. If you genuinely want agreement, this procedure may well offer the last opportunity, perhaps for many years, to achieve it. It will be a tragedy if that opportunity is squandered, but that seems to be the stark alternative.

He went on to point out that producing 'the elements of a settle-ment' would demand more than simply just listing the contentious issues: it would require co-operative efforts in defining solutions to those issues. Furthermore, he set a timetable for the discussions. He wanted each delegation to submit their draft Heads of Agreement, outlining the elements of a settlement in each of the three Strands, by the following Monday morning (19 October). The papers would then be discussed in individual delegation meetings with him on Monday, Tuesday, Wednesday and Thursday. By Friday morning he would circulate a proposal based on amalgamating their sugges-tions, and they would discuss it on Friday afternoon. The UUP, Alliance and, naturally, the two governments were positively keen on the idea. The DUP and SDLP grudgingly agreed. He finished by pleading with them to get down to serious negotiation:

> We need to go further than all the opening bids we have been hearing all these weeks and months, or else bring the whole process to an end ... Delegations should in their papers indicate how far they are really prepared to go ... The time for re-state-ment of opening positions is surely past.

On that note he adjourned the Committee for the day. With the formal session over, the Irish and British delegations met in the evening to try to work out an agreed position on North–South insti-tutions, in the hope that they might present a jointly sponsored draft Heads of Agreement to the Committee. But the arguments intruded even at this level, too. The Irish insisted on giving the North–South institutions an executive role. Nothing short of powerful cross-border institutions, they argued, would convince the Republic's electorate to vote for change to Articles Two and Three in a referendum. The British refused, convinced that any such powers would drive both Unionist parties out of the talks instantly. Yet again, Unionists – and the DUP in particular – had managed to manipulate the question of the Irish constitution into the first hurdle which every discussion must cross, even in their absence, before it could engage meaningfully about any aspect of the broader problem. Undoubtedly, some Unionists chose the tactic because of their belief that it was the most vital issue to be addressed, and the most important battle they must win. But equally obviously other Unionists were happy simply to use the issue as an effective block to any progress. Semantics were playing an increasing role in a revisitation of an earlier argument, as the Irish government insisted that they were able only to say that they *could* support a referendum, while Unionists demanded they say they *would* support one (*Irish Times* 17 October 1992).

When the Committee convened on Thursday morning, it was for a brief session only to endorse Ninian Stephen's plan to suspend the Committee in favour of bilateral meetings. The parties were happy to hand the responsibility over to him: 'Everyone was agreed,' recalls Thompson. 'They would just pass the ball to Sir Ninian and say, "Here you go, do your best, talk to all the parties and see if you can find a way through the mire."' Stephen spent the rest of the day in bilaterals with the DUP, the SDLP, Alliance and the Irish team. On Friday, he met with the UUP and the British. By Friday afternoon, he announced that he wanted more bilaterals with the four Northern parties on Monday and Tuesday next, and asked them to keep themselves available for further consultation for the rest of that week. The bilaterals brought to proceedings a focus that Stephen felt the larger discussions had lacked:

As far as negotiation was concerned, the interesting thing really was how impossible it would have been around the big table to have one party making a proposal, and the other party listening and then responding in any helpful way. Whereas to have one party in the room talking to us, and our then walking down the corridor to the other party to say, 'Look at this: what's your reaction?' really worked very well. The difference was quite extraordinary.

At the end of Friday's business, the UUP's Reg Empey addressed the press in upbeat manner, confirming his party's continuing commitment 'in the hope and expectation of a positive result'. His words sat uneasily with those of his party colleague Willie Ross who, 24 hours earlier, had criticized 'the long-lasting talking-shop in Stormont ... There are many who say we must keep talking no matter what. Quite frankly that is sheer nonsense. Talking for the sake of talking does no good whatsoever, and in fact does harm because it creates frustration and disillusion' (*Irish Times* 17 October 1992). Within the rather broad, occasionally unruly, church of the UUP, Ross came from the strand that was deeply sceptical of any high-profile talks which might lead to high-profile change. Led by Molyneaux himself, this grouping in the party tended to prefer low-level and small-scale alterations to existing arrangements. Thompson had noticed the internal UUP tensions, and in particular those between the leader and other delegates: 'Reg Empey was great, a terrific guy, very committed. Had he had a greater leadership role, we really could have got somewhere, I think.'

Over the weekend, Reynolds addressed the annual Wolfe Tone commemoration at Bodenstown, where he overtly linked the two key Strand 2 issues by asserting that constitutional change could only be achieved in return for strong cross-border institutions (*Irish Times* 19 October 1992). But by announcing also that he would be prepared to put the terms of any agreement to a referendum in the Republic if a simultaneous one was held in the North, he hoped to be seen as softening his stance on the Articles, since their alteration would naturally be part of the 'terms' of any agreement they might reach. Mayhew tried to talk up the remark, calling it 'encouraging' (*Irish Times* 21 October 1992), but the Unionists didn't bite, Maginnis dismissing it as nothing new (ibid. 20 October 1992).

For Monday and Tuesday of the following week, Stephen continued with his bilaterals at Stormont with the Northern parties and the British, trying to press them all to detailed positions on the core issues in the hope of producing a draft Heads of Agreement, or at least a positive progress report, before the talks deadline three weeks or so ahead. This was still 'in the hope', according to Thompson, that 'we might come through with some sort of a paper that wouldn't be a comprehensive settlement by any means, but at least might constitute agreement on the broad elements of a future settlement, something that could be picked up on and used for future progress.' While the British and Alliance remained relentlessly optimistic about achieving the goal of Heads of Agreement, the SDLP at least seemed to be setting their sights lower. On Wednesday 21 October Stephen travelled to Dublin to meet Wilson, Flynn and Molloy of the Irish government. Their conversation, they reported afterwards, was 'open and comprehensive' (*Irish Times* 22 October 1992). From Stephen's point of view, it was regrettable that Flynn was leading the delegation by this stage, since he personally suspected that Andrews held a less rigid stance. Nevertheless, he saw grounds for some optimism in a slight closing of the UUP–Dublin gap. Thompson too found the series of bilaterals:

> much more productive. There was a genuine willingness to find a way forward on the part of all. We had quite a few meetings with the DUP and I don't think there was much change in their position. But certainly the UUP were well engaged in the process, in particular the likes of Reg Empey were very helpful in trying to find a way forward.

On Thursday, everyone was back at Stormont, as Stephen changed his tack. This time, he chaired a series of trilateral meetings of the Irish government with, respectively, the UUP, SDLP and Alliance. (The DUP refused to meet the Irish delegation separately, saying they were waiting until they got a referendum commitment from them before there could be any meaningful talks.) During the day, he also met with the British delegation. Mayhew presented a draft Heads of Agreement, urging Stephen to adopt it as his amalgamated paper. The British encouraged Stephen to take the paper without attribution of its authorship, saying that it represented their best hope of what might be achievable among the Northern parties. But Stephen and Thompson both thought it quite unrealistic, reflecting more British frustration than any negotiating reality. Thompson remembers:

The British wanted quite desperately to get their proposal for Heads of Agreement on the table, and they were still hopeful there might be some way of doing that. Which was surprisingly naive, in our view. There was no way, we felt, that what the British had in mind as a Heads of Agreement could have received endorsement from the parties around the table ... The British were almost desperate to get an agreement out of this process. Mayhew wanted to be the Secretary that pulled off a solution, there's no question about that, and he did have hopes right up until the final phase.

They rejected the paper. But they continued the bilateral strategy on Friday. The attempt to get particular groupings focused on particular issues seemed to be proving useful. In particular, Thursday afternoon's and Friday morning's meetings between the UUP and the Dublin team on the issue of North–South institutions appeared positive. 'In the final phase,' Thompson remembers, 'there were moments, heady moments, where we thought we had a possible compromise between the Irish and the UUP: that was what we were looking for.'

While the position of the Irish government on establishing joint North–South institutions with executive powers was well known, the talking seemed to focus on a paper the UUP drew up which tried to sharpen up their concept of 'good-neighbourliness' into specific co-operation procedures on trade, transport, energy, industry, training, agriculture, tourism, and so on. But the limit of their suggestion seemed to be an Inter-Irish Relations Committee, which would be established by the new Northern government and would remain wholly subservient to it, and thus without any 'executive power'. Nonetheless, there seemed to be room for discussion. 'The real sticking point was,' says Stephen, 'should there be any executive power vested in the cross-border organisations? And there was great debate about what was meant by "executive power", and how it could be defined.'

By Friday, hints had emerged that there had been 'an interesting development' leading to 'worthwhile discussion' (*Irish Times* 28 October 1992). Of course, the DUP immediately accused Maginnis, Empey and other UUP negotiators of ceding, in Molyneaux's absence from Thursday's meeting, more than 'consultative' powers to the institutions. Paisley, himself in the southern states of the US on a preaching tour, telephoned the UUP leader on Thursday night to inform him that 'whatever the UUP delegates were discussing with [Irish] government ministers was unacceptable to the DUP' (ibid.). Thompson now admits to some misplaced hopes of detaching the UUP entirely from Paisley's party: 'I felt in the final part of the process that the UUP could have signed on to a document and accepted that the DUP would be opposing its entire contents. I think now that was over-optimistic.'

Other optimistic observers, however, were whispering that a compromise had been proposed:

> I do remember that the solution seemed to be to give them recommendatory power, to make recommendations to the government which could then implement them. If it was impossible for them to hold any executive power, then let the executive power be undertaken by the legislature giving effect to recommendations of the joint body. And that seemed a possible, feasible idea. (Stephen)

The Unionist parties went to war again over the weekend. The UUP Annual Conference included a great deal of criticism of the DUP. Ken Maginnis's comments on Saturday were typical: 'They've got the idea that they should wear not just a belt, but a belt and braces. And the sad thing is they haven't any trousers on. But don't worry, because if the Ulster Unionists succeed, they will be very willing to wear our trousers – they always have been in the past.' (*Irish Times* 26–27 October 1992). Sammy Wilson responded on Sunday, accusing some UUP negotiators of being 'Lundys [traitors]'. Maginnis dismissed him in a radio interview as 'Silly Sammy'. That evening, the DUP came back to accuse the UUP of 'bungling ineptness', defending its own stand in the talks and claiming that the UUP had broken a pact that no Unionist party would negotiate unilaterally. Sunday ended with an evening press statement from the UUP accusing the DUP of 'gross hypocrisy' with their latest charge, insisting that the DUP had already broken that pact by boycotting the talks (ibid).

On Monday, Mayhew again sent Sinn Fein a briefing on the talks. According to Sinn Fein papers, the 'British government representative' (in fact, a senior SIS officer) mentioned his previous talks briefings which had been very pessimistic. But this time, 'While that opinion had not changed, he pointed out that Ninian Stephen had improved the general climate. He provided the "Ninian Stephen" document as evidence of that' (Sinn Fein, 1993, p. 21). (The 'Ninian Stephen document' consists of an apparently internal British briefing document outlining recent strategy over the shift to a Heads of Agreement. For convenience, it is reproduced in full as Appendix 2.)

The rise in optimism was not only a British phenomenon. Small hopes of limited goals were being carefully nurtured. On Tuesday morning, 27 October, Stephen reconvened conventional bilaterals, expressing his hope of presenting a draft Heads of Agreement document for endorsement at a scheduled plenary on Friday of the following week. The bilaterals continued at Stormont for three days, and on Thursday culminated in a third UUP–Irish delegation meeting, a process that both sides apparently found sufficiently 'interesting' to want to continue (*Irish Times* 31 October 1992). Around the table, indeed, the meetings were generating some excitement, as Thompson recalls:

> We thought we had an emerging compromise on the nature of North–South structures, and this element of whether or not they should have executive authority. There was a moment where we actually felt that the UUP had signed on to a proposal that we knew would be acceptable to the Irish government.

That afternoon, Mayhew told the House of Commons that a Heads of Agreement document by 16 November (i.e., in two weeks) was 'a practical possibility' (*Irish Times* 30 October 1992).

The bilaterals continued throughout Friday. Stephen ended the week of what he saw as 'useful and productive' meetings with a brief plenary to gain approval for a full five days of further meetings the following week. The plan was agreed, since everyone (apart from the DUP, who were still refusing to engage with the Dublin delegation, and were increasingly suspicious of what the UUP were talking to Dublin about) seemed to value the smaller meetings. 'The bilaterals', one source told the *Irish Times*, 'have been far more useful than the sterile encounters in a committee around a table' (*Irish*

Times 31 October 1992). Everyone's attention was now focused on the impending deadline, just 17 days away. Heads of Agreement was a goal well short of a full three-stranded settlement, and even that seemed optimistic when the Unionist parties shortened the remaining time by declaring jointly that they would leave the talks after Tuesday 10 November, the date when the Conference Secretariat would begin preparations for the meeting. Suddenly, there was barely a week remaining. Tensions were not eased that night as the IRA exploded a bomb outside the British Cabinet Office in Whitehall, but their motivation had less to do with events at Stormont than with marking the last day in office of the outgoing head of Scotland Yard's Anti-Terrorist Branch. Ninian Stephen gave the opening address the next day to the annual conference of the Irish Bar Council, but refused diplomatically to be drawn on any of the legal arguments surrounding Irish constitutional change.

The intense round of bilaterals began on Monday morning, 2 November. But another serious tension was growing in the background. Andrews and Molloy were at Stormont in the morning for bilaterals with Stephen and with the SDLP. But they insisted on leaving after lunch, saying they needed to prepare for a vital cabinet meeting in the morning. In fact, a Tribunal of Inquiry into the Republic's beef industry had produced findings which were proving a deep embarrassment to the government, and rumours of a snap election were in the Dublin air. No one expected any Irish government representation at Stormont for the whole of the next day.

On Tuesday morning, as people digested the news of Bill Clinton's landslide victory in the US presidential election, it became apparent that the Irish delegation would not, indeed, be present, quite possibly for the entire week. This could prove very frustrating to any remaining hopes of progress, since the ongoing UUP–Dublin meetings were central to hopes of producing an agreed document by Friday. But bilaterals continued among those present, and some contacts were made with the Irish government by telephone. Nonetheless, events in the Irish Republic could not have come at a worse time, as Thompson recalls how close the two sides were coming in a quid pro quo that would have seen a Unionist concession on executive power in return for an Irish agreement to hold a referendum:

Things were moving pretty quickly in that period. We thought we had a UUP agreement to an expression of the degree to which this North–South entity would have executive powers. There was a fair bit of excitement on the part of the Irish as well, and on the part of Flynn in particular. I remember at one late-night meeting we had in Dublin, he was saying 'Yes! We're going to crack this!' and getting really quite excited ... But the UUP quickly pulled back from it. Either we were too optimistic in our interpretation of what we thought we had, or as soon as we put it into black and white they pulled back from it.

And he also points out that it was not just the UUP for whom such agreement proved a step too far:

But it was all too much for the Irish delegation. They were too close to an election, and I think they had taken a political decision that they could not go into an election with a concession to the Unionists on constitutional reform – they just couldn't do that. So they withdrew from what was emerging.

Things only got worse on Wednesday. A crucial debate on the ratification of the Maastricht Treaty was scheduled for that night in the House of Commons, and the attendance of all MPs – British and Northern Irish – was obligatory. That evening a rumour circulated around Westminster that an hour before the vote Mayhew summoned to his office three UUP MPs, among them Ken Maginnis, to discuss establishing a Northern Ireland Select Committee (a long-cherished goal of Molyneaux) in return for a pro-Conservative UUP vote over Maastricht. No deal, however, was done, but most Unionists supported the Conservatives, and Major scraped home with a three-vote majority. Meanwhile in the Dail, Andrews and the government refused calls to postpone the Conference meeting to provide more negotiating time to compensate for the loss of the week or so caused by the crisis in Ireland.

On Thursday 5 November, Irish officials took the places of their ministers in bilaterals, as it was announced in Dublin that there would be an election in three weeks, on 25 November. With all the disruptions of the week, the goal of the talks had been much reduced from a Heads of Agreement document to merely something much vaguer which would, according to one delegate, 'keep the show on the road, bind the process together with a view to a resumption in the future' (*Irish Times* 6 November 1992).

Andrews, Wilson and Flynn made their first collective appearance of the week at Stormont on Friday morning. But they had come merely to argue that the talks must be concluded that very day, or else suspended until after the Irish election. Angry words were exchanged, as the Unionists demanded that everyone stay in the talks until next Tuesday. Dublin, supported only by the SDLP, argued that a suspension would be fair, since it had at least technically happened in March, when the initial opening meeting of renewed talks had only met to agree a suspension to allow for a British election. The day's plenary session was at first postponed and then cancelled, and the day of bilaterals ran on in 'tetchy exchanges' (*Irish Times* 7 November 1992) before an angry Irish government delegation agreed to return for a final plenary the following Tuesday. The goal now had been reduced merely to reaching a 'joint statement' which would underwrite a resumption of talks at a later date. But Stephen defends the caution of that approach: 'We thought talks would be resumed [later]. And therefore there was a strong feeling that very little should be said, because anything that might be said could be so easily turned into a stumbling block on resumption.'

A final day of bilaterals was held on Monday 9 November, again with officials representing Dublin, as Stephen struggled on to reach some agreed summary of the progress and positions to date. A new draft paper by the UUP was rejected by most participants, and it was clear to all now that they had fallen far short of their limited goal for the three weeks of bilaterals. Indeed, most delegates were by now more interested in manoeuvring to avoid blame for the collapse of talks, rather than in any last-minute breakthrough.

8
Endgame: 'The Riddle of the Strands': November

On Tuesday afternoon 10 November, Irish ministers arrived for a brief plenary in which a statement was approved by all parties announcing the end of the talks. For all the argument that had preceded it, the statement was an anodyne affair of little more than 500 words, of which only around 150 words addressed any question of progress achieved or of future dialogue. 'All parties accepted that nothing would be finally agreed in any of the three strands of the Talks until everything was agreed in the Talks as a whole. We report that the Talks did not reach this stage.' It was depressingly little to show for six months of work. Mark Brennock commented cogently:

> What was initially a search for a historic new agreement became a search for heads of agreement, for elements of agreement, for a 'soft landing' to allow for an early resumption of talks and, finally, for an agreed statement. (*Irish Times* 11 November 1992)

In the negotiating room, the mood was sombre – 'complete demoralisation', as one Alliance delegate put it. Indeed, Addie Morrow of the Alliance party 'burst into tears. I found that very moving, and it had quite an impact on the Irish delegation as well' (Thompson). Only the Irish delegation came out of Stormont making positive noises. 'I don't see the talks having broken down,' said Andrews, while Flynn insisted there remained 'real potential for agreement' (*Irish Times* 11 November 1992). Mayhew tried to be upbeat too, but the Northern parties had a different view. 'It is a rather sad day for the people of Northern Ireland,' said Alderdice. 'It is no great surprise, but a matter of considerable disappointment. We didn't run out of time – we didn't find a situation in which compromise was possible' (ibid.). Both Unionist parties conceded that there had been some benefits, in particular that the parties' positions had been identified and refined. But they and Alliance accused the SDLP of starting from a knowingly impossible negotiating position in Strand 1, and then refusing to move an inch. Hume rejected the criticism, seeing the experience as a clarifying one which laid a sound basis for further work. But Paisley, forthright to the last, blamed the SDLP for intransigence over the devolution formula, and Dublin for intransigence over Articles Two and Three. 'These talks are dead,' he declared (*Irish Times* 11 November 1992).

The following day, preparations began at the Maryfield Secretariat for the 16 November Conference meeting. In the House of Commons, Mayhew's statement to parliament was upbeat, expressing hope of an early resumption and pleading for no recriminations. But in the ensuing debate, Unionist MPs were all critical of, as they perceived it, Dublin's uncompromising stance. Maginnis complained that the Irish government 'made not a single, solitary compromise', while SDLP MPs criticized what they termed 'the three unionist parties' for being unable to transcend the confines of Northern Ireland in the attempt to devise institutional arrangements (*Irish Times* 12 November 1992).

An official statement from the Irish government insisted that the first essential condition for future progress had been achieved: 'Each tradition has been able for the first time to define for the other the full dimensions of the sincerely held positions which must be reconciled' (*Irish Times* 12 November 1992). Stephen was initially surprised at this perception, but later agreed that this was a small but vital piece of progress:

> The leaders of the various parties, I think, ceased to regard each other, and the ministers of the Crown and Ireland, as demonised figures, and came to acknowledge them as human beings. A very strong factor in it all was sitting and listening to the other fellow's version of the past, and not agreeing with it by any means, but realising that the other fellow actually believed in his version. In litigation, when you get the parties together, they've

never really understood the argument of the other side. But when they hear what the argument is, quietly in a room as distinct from a court, they realise there is some substance to it. It was the same thing, I think, with the Unionists generally and the SDLP.

But in the Republic, just two weeks away from a general election, the talks rapidly became a campaign issue, as Fianna Fail and the Progressive Democrats (with help from Fine Gael) criticized each other's role, one side claiming that Reynolds's hardline stance on the Articles had been a 'public display of bad faith towards Unionists', the other expressing shock that the confidential talks should be abused to become 'a political football in the general election' (*Irish Times* 13 November 1992). Thompson bitterly regretted the timing of events in the Republic:

> The concession over Articles Two and Three was often tantalisingly close. I always felt that if the Irish government were prepared to move from *could* to *would*, that could be a circuitbreaker for getting concessions from the Unionists about the nature of the North–South structures. I always felt the Irish were often almost on the point of being prepared to sign up to that form of words. But certainly not ahead of an election. We were very close to that point, but all hope evaporated as the election got closer.

The UUP's Chris McGimpsey summed up the whole process succinctly in an *Irish Times* article three days after the final plenary:

> The same learning experience took place during the first phase of the talks under the tutelage of Peter Brooke. We each learned a little about the other, and the scene was set for the Mayhew talks ... To say the talks have failed is, of course, accurate on one level. No agreement has emerged, and that is a pity. However, if we still lack the physics to reach a settlement, at least the chemistry has improved dramatically ... With a bit of luck we will soon recommence talks in some format or other. (*Irish Times* 13 November 1992)

But he also warned: 'In the meantime, the paramilitaries within Northern Ireland will have a field day. The sooner constitutional politicians take them on, the better' (ibid.).

McGimpsey's warning was soon fulfilled. The day his article appeared, a huge IRA bomb devastated the mainly protestant town of Coleraine. The following day, an Ulster Freedom fighters' (UFF) gun attack on a Belfast betting shop left three Catholics dead and eight injured. The IRA killed an RUC reserve constable, and a UFF statement warned Republicans to expect heavy casualties.

As the Australians reported dejectedly to their government, the 'riddle of the Strands' had proved insoluble this time around. From the first, its aim of a comprehensive settlement had been extremely ambitious for a six-month negotiation. The intractability of the core issue of the Border, moreover, had produced irreconcilable positions and a general refusal to consider accommodation: 'compromise is as much of a sin in Northern Ireland as capitulation', they noted. Finally, their diagnosis suggested that there was a lack of incentive to look for such compromise, since no side was hurting sufficiently under the prevailing circumstances.

Only Stephen and Thompson emerged from the process unscathed, comprehensively appreciated and complimented on their contribution. Major and Reynolds wrote jointly to the Australian government:

> We consider the dialogue that has taken place hitherto has been valuable, and further dialogue is both necessary and desirable. We welcome the fact that all the parties agree with this judgement ... We believe it is right to relieve your government and Sir Ninian of any obligation. If agreement is reached on the basis of future talks, we hope it might be possible to call once more on your services.

There had been a learning process. There had been familiarization. There had been clarification of positions. There had been 'chemistry lessons'. There had been symbolic breakthroughs. But there was never a meeting of minds. Twice in two years now, the politicians had sat down to negotiate towards a settlement, and failed spectacularly to get within miles of that goal. The same doubt that had beset observers of the 1991 Brooke talks was still in many minds: where was the political will to move beyond point-scoring and rhetoric into real creative negotiation?

After the collapse of the Brooke talks, it was the Unionist parties who shouldered the popular blame for failure. This time, whatever the feelings of participants, some of the blame fell on Hume and the SDLP. The Unionists, in particular, saw his rejection of the Strand 1 devolution formula as a sign that he was not seriously seeking a real deal. It is too simplistic a conclusion to draw about this complex man who was, after all, engaged in a much more complex game than anyone else realized at the time. But certainly, in comparing the 1991 and 1992 talks, the Unionists (or at least the UUP) looked much more serious second time around, where the SDLP seemed slightly insecure even with the banking principle which Hume himself had devised. We cannot doubt the SDLP's commitment to dialogue and to a settlement, but at important times in the 1992 talks they demonstrated a degree of prevarication and stubbornness to match that of the UUP.

9
Conclusion: Northern Ireland: 'Just a Step Along the Way'

In overall political terms, as in the public view, the Mayhew talks failed, as the Brooke talks a year previously had also failed. The talks agenda expressed the goal of an overall settlement comprising all three strands or relationships. Clearly, no such ambitious result was forthcoming. Indeed, since no single strand reached anything like a definite conclusion, it is hard to claim even a partial success.

But if we take a longer view, and see the talks as another stage in an ongoing process, then we can see a more positive outcome: the agenda of the Brooke talks was taken further, genuine engagement took place at several points over substantive issues, the detail and implications of various agenda items were examined in depth. And undoubtedly every party gained insight into the feasibility of their own demands, into the actuality of their opponents' positions, and into the negotiating style and approach of various parties and individuals. Additionally, the uneasy cross-table relationship, the personal chemistry between participants, developed significantly. Coming out of the Mayhew talks, every party had gained significant further understanding of each other and of the process of negotiating, whether or not they were happy with that new knowledge. The effects of the Brooke talks were reinforced. The habit of dialogue was more deeply embedded and, to some extent, although there was genuine disappointment and frustration at the failure, there was a deeper recognition that dialogue must be the way forward. To paraphrase Molyneaux, what they had now done twice, they might do more successfully a third time.

It is enlightening to look at each party to the talks in terms of their agenda as they began, the style or role they utilized during the process, the gains or concessions they made or considered, and their position at the end in terms of that initial agenda. Such examination reveals a diversity of goals, approaches and agendas which, while certainly complicating events at the time, helps to explain and clarify both the advances made and the difficulties encountered along the way.

The Alliance Party

The Alliance Party stands out among the delegations as the one most motivated towards an agreement. This is no surprise, and no change from the previous year: although pragmatically supporting a position close in many respects to moderate Unionism, Alliance were alone in entering the talks specifically in order to make compromises. The Alliance position, in a broad sense, was to find a compromise based on pragmatic realities (e.g., the fact that a majority of Northern Ireland's population wanted to remain in the UK for the time being), rather than to look for a specific quid pro quo between themselves and another. Further, their pragmatism meant that they constantly proposed a middle-ground position, rather than, like the others, trying to protect a traditional position and win concessions from a traditional opponent. Seeing themselves in something of a middle position among the Northern parties, they aimed rather to forge a compromise which would suit everyone. In this sense, they contributed more perhaps to the *process* of the talks than to the design of an *outcome* in any particular strand. Thompson acknowledged this role as a very positive one:

> Often the role Alliance played was most important procedurally. They could always be counted on to back the chair, with a compromise proposal to keep things going, or to come in with a helpful intervention. They were extremely helpful to us.

Alliance's contribution was thus more process-oriented. They oiled the creaking wheels of dialogue. 'The Alliance did seem to have good relations with the SDLP and the Unionists,' remarked Stephen. Because of their middle-ground stance, they were seen as less threatening to the other participants and thus were one party who could approach others, stimulate unofficial interaction, shuttle between delegations as message-carriers, and use interventions at the table, particularly by Alderdice, to suggest compromises or alternatives at points of blockage.

But this role must not be overstated: Alliance were not strong enough – either electorally or in terms of delivering a constituency – to influence any other party against its will or to offer rewards in return for concessions. In that sense, Alliance had no bargaining chips at all, compared to the other parties. Their central aim was to reach compromise, rather than to satisfy a partial or communal viewpoint. Their approach was to represent pragmatism, and to try to encourage others to do so in a co-operative search for compromise. Only in the sense that they were 'polite Unionists', as one SDLP delegate dubbed them, could they offer any kind of moderating influence on Unionist positions, and even then this was slight. In effect, their goal was to reach a compromise on virtually every item under discussion, and while this was a positive contribution to the dialogue process, as a political aim it was largely unachieved. Certainly, individual members of Alliance took the breakdown of the talks in November as a much greater disappointment than did other delegates. No one was truly optimistic in November about a restart, but Alliance seemed much more gloomy for the future than anyone. Whether they naively held higher initial hopes for progress than others, the let-down was much more of a disaster in Alliance eyes. Eileen Bell's reaction was typical of the party:

> I was really disappointed at the end of the Mayhew talks. I remember sitting with a drink on the steps of the inside of the Assembly building with Jeremy Hanley. And he put his two arms around me, because I was really, really emotional that night. I was really disappointed that at the end of it all, the only thing we had to show really was that we still didn't like each other, we still didn't trust each other.

Of course, simply being there was in a way an achievement in itself for Alliance, given their small electoral base. They would have been rather upset themselves to be described as 'polite unionists', but they were seen by Paisley as enough of a troublesome moderating influence on Unionism during the Brooke talks that he had tried to have them excluded this time around. Indeed, during the winter of 1991, the DUP had been scathing and insulting about Alliance's perceived inability to protect a Unionist point of view. But, then, that was not their aim. To be there, and to oil the processional wheels to the extent that they were able was, if disappointingly short of a full settlement, nevertheless a tangible achievement for the Alliance Party. In essence, a successful process – and, within reason, whatever the shape of the eventual settlement – was the Alliance goal. The strength which allowed them to take the middle ground of compromise almost all the time was also their weakness: that middle-ground position by definition meant that they did not have a significant constituency of either unionism or nationalism whom they could deliver in the event of a deal.

The Democratic Unionist Party

What then of the DUP agenda? Clearly from the start it was protectionist: defined, articulated and defended volubly by Paisley. Sammy Wilson gave an interesting insight into the party's preparations for the 1991 talks with Brooke:

> I remember the day in the Stormont Hotel when we actually sat down to [prepare for the talks]. One group in the party were saying, 'Look, let's go in with something that really there's no way they're going to accept, and then we've got something to bargain with.' And there was another group who said, 'Look, we've got a time limit. Let's go in there with our bottom line and show our hand immediately.' ... Those of us who took the [second] line got pilloried in the party afterwards.

From the start of the Brooke talks, there had thus been doubts about which faction of the party was dictating tactics. A year later, those doubts had been resolved. Second time around, there was little evidence of any preparedness to lay out realistic negotiating positions or to consider compromise. Paisley was always conscious of the hardline wing of his party, represented most clearly by the likes of Westminster MP, Free Presbyterian minister and country and western gospel singer, Revd William McCrea. McCrea had hotly refused to be any part of Strand 2 dealings, because Strand 1 had not achieved enough progress on devolution for him to warrant the risk of talking to Dublin in Strand 2. Despite the involvement of more liberal or pragmatic members of the delegation, like Wilson, Campbell and Robinson for example, Paisley was personally more comfortable with McCrea's hardline position. Indeed, UUP delegates talked of their frustration that when any proposal was offered to the DUP for consideration, the reaction was always, 'Well, first we'll have to get it past the Doc and Willie [Paisley and McCrea]'. It is fair to say that the McCrea position of needing a satisfactory conclusion to Strand 1 before any concessions in Strand 2 might be considered, quickly became the leader's, and the party's, basic position. Without a devolution formula under their belt, they saw little positive attraction in any other Strand. And thus from the very start of Strand 2, the DUP was only interested in winning unilateral concessions from the opposition (specifically, over Articles Two and Three) or in scoring points, and not in any real two-sided deal-making. Indeed, much of their activity in Strand 2 involved finding reasons not to do a deal. In this respect, Padraig Flynn was unwittingly of great assistance: his arrogant manner and his ministerial annoyance at being so roughly treated by a mere regional party, confirmed many DUP suspicions about the nature of the Irish Republic and its government. The personality clash between him and Paisley worked very effectively for the DUP agenda.

The DUP had simple, if immutable, goals. First and foremost, they wanted a devolved administration that included the SDLP but that enshrined the old democratic principle of the rights of the majority. Clearly, the SDLP and Dublin – not to mention most other participants, including the British government – were not going to run with such an idea in Strand 1. But as with Flynn in Strand 2, the SDLP again played into Paisley's hands by producing a proposal that, to Unionist eyes, significantly undermined the sovereignty of Northern Ireland by permitting Dublin and Brussels to participate through the Panel in the government of the North. Paisley and Robinson were undoubtedly quite honest in their outrage at this concept – as indeed were the UUP for the most part – but it also effectively gave them an excuse to avoid meaningful engagement while accusing the SDLP of doing exactly that.

Nonetheless, it must be acknowledged that the party – and in particular the Robinson faction – did engage seriously in the discussions around the Strand 1 *Possible Outline Framework*. Robinson tried hard to push the Sub-Committee to a conclusion, and his initials went on the 3 June draft. But when the pressure ultimately failed to win Hume over to the *Framework*, the party seemed to accept this as confirmation that no gains would be forthcoming. From that point onward, they gave up any positive efforts, and reverted instead to Paisley's tried, tested, and comfortably familiar strategy of producing 'tension on demand'.

Their second, and perhaps overall, goal was to attack the Anglo-Irish Agreement. Despite the fact that, since its signing in 1985, the Agreement had proved resilient to their best efforts, and had embedded itself in – and even significantly shaped – the political context of Northern Ireland, it remained an outrage to Unionists in general but to the DUP in particular. Not only had Unionists felt excluded from the negotiation of the Agreement (unlike the SDLP, who had worked busily with the Dublin government), but the Agreement had imposed unacceptable arrangements upon them: 'foreign' Irish civil servants serviced the Agreement from a base in Belfast, and Dublin had a formal channel of input into the government of Northern Ireland through the regular Anglo-Irish Conference meetings. Thus, one of the Unionists' first preconditions for talks with Brooke had been a suspension of the Agreement, and a readiness to negotiate a replacement for it. The suspension had been whittled down to simply the suspension of Conference meetings during negotiations. In everyone's eyes but the Unionists', that was nothing more than a fig leaf. Everyone knew that suspending a few meetings neither cancelled Dublin's co-operation with London nor threatened the Agreement in any real way. By the time of the Mayhew talks, although the UUP still agreed with Paisley about the need to suspend meetings, it was the DUP alone who still saw the talks as a way to attack the Agreement, and who perceived the Conference suspensions as any substantive blow to its effectiveness. This perception remained with them. Walking out of the talks, despite the blame they would shoulder, would have been the most effective way of protecting the DUP position, had they not still seen prolonged, if aimless, negotiations as a means of undermining the Agreement. That may be the main reason they stayed at the talks as long as they did, and indeed was no doubt used internally as an argument in favour of at least some engagement with Dublin.

The other reason for their remaining at the table, of course, was to undermine the possibility of any settlement. They remained supremely convinced of their importance in the political process, and took confidence from the fact that neither they nor any other party really believed a deal could be struck without their participation. (It was certainly Stephen's understanding that, awkward as the DUP might be, they were essential to a deal.) Having the DUP outside and opposed would, at that time in Unionist political development, have fundamentally undermined, if not rendered practically impossible, the sustained implementation of any new political structures. And Paisley knew this well. In that light, the sensible tactic in Strand 2 was to demand wholesale the only thing they were really interested in – the removal of Dublin's territorial claim to the North – and to go on the attack over everything else. So they elevated their demand into a precondition, which made its granting all the more unlikely. Thus, the DUP would claim an equally good day's work if they managed to weaken Dublin's argument over the Articles, or if they simply managed to drive obstructive wedges between or among other parties. For Paisley, the agenda was thus largely a defensive one: give away nothing, try to undermine the opponents. And so attack was the best form of defence. Very few, if any, concessions were at that time sellable in any way to the 'Doc and Willie' constituency of the DUP; the party's job therefore was to protect the current position at all costs, since any concession was, in Stephen's words, as bad as capitulation in DUP eyes. Since almost any change that came out of the talks would be, by definition and in advance, for the worse according to the DUP perspective, they held determinedly to an ultra-protectionist agenda well summed up in the old unionist slogan, 'No Surrender!' Thompson recalls in stark words the cynicism bred of the DUP's behaviour:

It became apparent fairly early in the process, at least to Sir Ninian and me, that it was going to be impossible to produce an agreement that the DUP would be part of, that whatever concessions one might be able to wring from the Irish, it wouldn't be sufficient to get the DUP on board ... First of all, we thought they would never get the precondition they were looking for [on Irish constitutional change]. And we were never really convinced that if they did get that precondition, they would then talk turkey on the other blockages ... They used to say, and in writing, that if the Irish were prepared to make that concession, then their attitude would change entirely. But nobody believed that!

In short, if they couldn't get what they wanted in Strand 1 – and undoubtedly their expectations were unrealistic there – they would make sure that all engagement was to no avail. They entered the process with the goals of weakening the Agreement, asserting the Unionist majority in any devolved structure, and changing the Irish constitution. When the latter two proved unattainable, they fell back on the first – a goal which they and the UUP had sought co-operatively as a team in 1991, but which by now the UUP had begun to realise was an illusion and a minor distraction.

The Ulster Unionist Party

To some degree, the two Unionist parties shared the same aims in the talks. But in general the UUP's position was less intransigent, at least to the degree where they were prepared to consider concessions if the gains were commensurable. There was the semi-external goal of undermining the Anglo-Irish Agreement simply by maintaining its symbolic suspension as long as the dialogue continued. But the UUP, second time around with Mayhew, had realised that this was indeed more symbolic than substantive. It became little more for them than a side-benefit, since this time the UUP, at least in the early stages, actually saw the possibility of deal-making. The argument of the two governments, of course, was that the best way to get rid of the Agreement was to carry through the talks to a successful conclusion, since that would include the Strand 3 business of negotiating a replacement for the Agreement. Having tried unsuccessfully to wreck it by non-compliance and symbolism for several years since its signing and also in the Brooke talks, the UUP were this time more believing in the value of negotiation in general, and in its use to replace, rather than simply remove, the Agreement.

Even Molyneaux, the arch-sceptic of the Brooke talks, who had continually dismissed such high-profile direct negotiations as a 'high-wire act', saw some value in a second attempt. As Alderdice recalls: 'I saw a very different Molyneaux in the 1992 talks, totally different from the Brooke talks. ... In my view he was prepared to do business, he was prepared to take risks.'

The UUP leader nevertheless maintained the personal *modus operandi* which he had operated the previous year: he himself took a back-seat in the negotiations, often absent from the table, having delegated Empey and Maginnis as the respective negotiation leaders for Strands 1 and 2. Of course, he held regular meetings with his teams, often at the end of the negotiating day, and was a central player in policy formation. But, in keeping with his tight-lipped and minimalist style of leadership, he left the action largely to others. 'We did try to engage Molyneaux, I know, in a couple of [bilateral and trilateral] meetings in the final phase,' Thompson remarked. 'And I know that the British were keen that we try to engage him in the process.' But Molyneaux proved impervious to such approaches. 'He took almost no part. It was very disappointing, I thought,' reflected Stephen. While this system worked well initially, there were occasions in the later Strand 2 stages when differences opened up between the leader and his chieftains, most usually when the latter were looking more amenable to agreement.

Molyneaux had always been sceptical of negotiated solutions. His own preferred approach was to tinker with the legislative mechanisms of government at Westminster, to produce minimal change in Northern Ireland. Indeed, he remained strongly wedded to the idea of integration, a solution which proposed making Northern Ireland a full part of the British central and regional government systems, ('as British as Finchley', as one-time integrationist Margaret Thatcher had described it). Thus Northern Ireland would be fully integrated into the British structures – no devolution, no separate treatment from that of, say, Yorkshire. Integration had largely had its day as a cause in Unionism, not least because most Unionists had realized that it was no longer on offer from Britain under any circumstances. But Molyneaux, for all that he tried to accommodate all factions of the broad church of his party, remained nostalgically wedded to the idea. It could only serve to weaken his belief in the possibility of any devolved outcome to

Strand 1. But undoubtedly Molyneaux's grip on his party was less vicelike than Paisley's, and he was at least prepared to consider party points of view other than his own personal preferences.

In the Strand 1 talks, the UUP were obviously prepared to make concessions. While their initial position on Strand 1 was a limited form of power-sharing which would still have worked to favour Unionism strongly, it became clear that it was negotiable. Even while they found the SDLP's Panel proposal initially abhorrent, nonetheless this too they were prepared to negotiate over, however grudgingly. It was John Hume who claimed to have invented the banking principle ('nothing is agreed until everything is agreed') specifically to reassure Unionists in 1991, and the UUP do seem to have actually embraced it in a more positive light in the 1992 talks. They could go as far as offering a specific, serious and genuine deal to the SDLP in Strand 1, secure in the knowledge that if they were faced with too high a price in Strand 2, their refusal to agree in every Strand would still scupper the whole deal, and wipe out any concessions offered.

The UUP strategy was to view Strand 1 as the place to make as many gains as possible, and Strand 2 as a process of limiting concessions as far as possible. But they did see the potential gain in Strand 2 for changing Articles Two and Three, and had the self-confidence among themselves and, crucially, among their voters to go to Dublin to try to win concessions from the Irish government, without losing face simply by crossing the border. While the DUP saw Strand 2 as something that could only end in tears, the UUP were, despite their scepticism, prepared to test the waters, as long as they had the lifebelt of the banking principle to pull them back to shore if the currents proved treacherous.

Strand 1 ground to a standstill over the UUP-sponsored formula of which the SDLP, without altogether rejecting, withheld its approval, subject to the progress of matters more central to their concerns in Strand 2. The UUP must have known that the formula was not yet dead in the water. Indeed, it was clear to all that the price of the SDLP's espousing of the devolution formula would be significant Unionist and British concessions in Strand 2. Once Strand 2 had opened, however, it rapidly became clear that the DUP was mostly interested in obstruction, and the Irish government were holding a very hard line on the Agreement and on the Articles.

Rapidly Molyneaux lost whatever enthusiasm he had initially entertained:

> Molyneaux was always distant and uncommitted, I thought, always ... We suspected that Molyneaux had made a political judgement early on in Strand 2 that the process wasn't going to lead anywhere, and that his reputation wasn't going to be tainted as a consequence. (Thompson)

And yet, there were flickers of movement in the UUP camp during the last weeks of the talks. When Stephen abandoned the committee structure in favour of direct meetings with one or at most two delegations, glimpses of light appeared in both the Dublin and Ulster Unionist positions. While they remained locked in an argument over whether the Irish government 'could' or 'would' initiate a referendum to change Articles Two and Three, the discussions were serious. In Thompson's words, 'We had a lot of argument over that. But nevertheless the UUP agreed that it was progress, and a sufficient basis on which to continue talking.' However, it was clear now that any sign of softening in the UUP position merely provoked serious attacks from the DUP, who had now firmly ruled out any possibility of progress and were happy to snipe menacingly at their rivals for unionist votes. This left the UUP very little room for manoeuvre that did not risk potentially damaging accusations of sell-out from the DUP.

In general, it could be said that the UUP approach to the talks was a predominantly defensive one: first and foremost to concede as little as possible, and only thereafter to consider the potential benefits of any gains still possible within that limitation. As can be identified within most of the delegations, of course, there were differing internal UUP opinions. The infamous breadth of opinion within the party had often proved both a burden and a boon in past times. While Molyneaux exercised a conservative whip, albeit from a back seat, negotiators like Empey, Maginnis, McGimpsey and others clearly exercised a moderating influence on him. 'There's no doubting Ken Maginnis' genuineness,' recalls Thompson, 'even though he was often longwinded and sometimes – unwittingly, I'm sure – took things off course ... [In the bilateral stage] the likes of Reg Empey were very helpful in trying to find a way forward.'

Their initial agenda was protectionist and sceptical. Their method was, however, to engage in largely meaningful and committed discussion, and gradually, even as Molyneaux grew more sceptical, most of the key delegates were drawn in to the process of negotiation and its potential for progress. At the very last gasp of the talks, the UUP seemed ready to consider a major concession on the power of North–South institutions:

> We thought we had an emerging compromise on the nature of a North–South structure, and whether or not it should have executive authority. There was a moment where we actually felt that the UUP had signed up to a proposal that we knew would be acceptable to the Irish government. But they quickly pulled back from it. Either we were too optimistic in the interpretation we had put on what we thought we had, or as soon as we put it in black and white they pulled back from it. (Thompson)

The exact degree to which the DUP had by then successfully reduced the room for manoeuvre of the UUP is impossible to quantify. But undoubtedly such attacks from behind made it all the more difficult and politically dangerous for the UUP negotiators to continue in meaningful dialogue with those before them. The DUP was still their only real rival for unionist votes, and the UUP did not feel strong enough to compete directly with the arch-rival on such sensitive ground. Interestingly, just five years later, with the rise of the loyalist political parties, it did prove possible and fruitful to continue serious negotiation in the DUP's absence, and subsequently to try to implement the outcome despite their antagonism. But in 1992, the exclusion of Paisley was still seen on all sides as attractive but impossible.

The Social Democratic and Labour Party

One overall trend that differentiates in general between the Nationalists and the Unionists is the balance of positive and negative approaches to the negotiations. It is pretty fair to say in broad terms that Unionists came to the table with a defensive or negative attitude: opinions ranged from believing an outcome impossible to fearing any possible outcome. In contrast, Nationalists were, in general, possessed of a more positive attitude, one that looked at the negotiations as a potential means of progress, as a process that would not actually damage the Nationalist position in any material way, but which on the contrary held the potential for substantive gains: hands on the levers of government in Belfast, and new structures for political co-operation across the border which would, by definition, leach some of the political power away from northern Unionism and into the broader Irish context. It is a reasonable generalization to say that the Northern Ireland context dictated that any negotiations would involve mainly Unionist concessions and Nationalist gains. So where the Unionists had limited goals from the outset, most of which were defensive, the SDLP and Dublin saw themselves as on course towards a goal and keen to make progress.

That said, there remains the shock of the initial SDLP proposal in Strand 1. Even the Dublin government had warned them that the UUP would find the externally appointed Panel unpalatable. And yet they went ahead. There could be few among the SDLP's experienced heads who expected anything but immediate Unionist rejection. The DUP's Sammy Wilson recalls the Unionist reaction to the proposal:

> When John Hume came in with his proposals about a Commission with six people, three from here and one from the Republic and one from England and one from Europe and everything else, we honestly couldn't believe it ... Really we thought it was some kind of sick joke at the start.

But if we assume, fairly, that the SDLP priority was to make gains in Strand 2, it makes sense to interpret their initial Strand 1 proposal as something to be reduced only as the possibilities of Strand 2 progress were realized. Indeed, there were several of the SDLP negotiators, led in particular by Durkan, who were prepared to sign up to the Unionist-proposed formula for devolution, until Hume vetoed it. A DUP delegate takes up the story of 3 June:

> Peter Robinson and I went up to get a cup of tea. And on the way up, Peter said to me: 'I think we've got them.' And Jeremy Hanley was there with a big smile on his face. I think Hanley was all

ready to go down and just sign up for his knighthood, because there had been agreement between all the parties. And we felt that with that substantial progress, you could move on to Strand 2.

But next morning, Hume appeared in the back corridor, and he'd a face like thunder. Mark Durkan had phoned Hume late the previous night [about the agreement] and I don't remember his exact words to me, but it was to the effect, 'I got my balls chewed off last night'. He said he'd phoned Hume, and Hume had gone buck daft and in fact refused to let any of the three [Sub-Committee members] back anywhere near the Sub-Committee. Hume just dispensed with it, and literally overnight it was scrapped.

We need to take the partisan tone of the tale with a pinch of DUP salt, although there is no reason to deny the gist. The simplest explanation is that Hume was prepared to go close to a Strand 1 deal, but not actually strike one, until they reached a similar point in Strand 2. So the Panel proposition can perhaps best be explained as an attempt, conscious or otherwise within the party, to take a more hardline initial position in order to turn it into a possible bargaining chip down the line. In the Northern Irish context, this was an entirely acceptable tactic. Moreover, the SDLP were, numerically and ideologically, outnumbered in Strand 1, and no doubt felt great pressure from time to time from all the other participants. It may have led them to act a little more defensively than necessary. Certainly once Strand 2 opened and they had their close partners from Dublin involved, the balance was somewhat redressed.

So it can fairly be said that the main SDLP goals going into negotiation were to develop strong Strand 2 structures for the joint North–South exercise of power, and in return to accede to a devolution formula for Strand 1 if calculations proved that it was worth it. They took widespread criticism for refusing to accept the June deal in Strand 1, but stuck to their guns. The strategy only really began to display its logic as Strand 2 unfolded. But of course it never unfolded far enough to satisfy them. In Strand 2, even the SDLP were partially sidelined by the UUP–Dublin focus of so much of the dialogue, and could only watch Dublin in an advisory and supportive manner as they tackled Unionism across the table.

There is no reason whatever to suspect Hume and his party of anything short of genuine commitment to the process. But it is hard to believe that the leader, at least, thought that these negotiations could bring a complete package. Otherwise, why was he in continuing discussion with Adams? It would be more accurate to say that the SDLP commitment to a comprehensive peace settlement was unquestionable, but that their definition of that comprehensiveness was broader than just this particular exercise in dialogue. Specifically, Hume had realized that the exclusive nature of the talks, rejecting any political party linked to violence, circumscribed their ability to address the concerns of violent Republicanism. And so there could only ever be a partial solution around that particular table. Thompson recalled an insightful conversation with Hume following the final formal session in November:

> I remember him almost patting me on the back and saying, 'Don't worry. It was meant to be. This is just a step along the way on the path of a larger process.' I always had the feeling that Hume knew there would eventually have to be an extra seat at the table [for Sinn Fein] for a real settlement. And he was always aware that we would need that other player if we were to pull it off.

Another explanation of the Panel proposal in Strand 1, then, is that it was also a lurch away from what Unionists could accept specifically to be more attractive to Sinn Fein. This is not for a moment to suggest that Gerry Adams was about to sign up at that stage for any such variation on a partitionist solution; but perhaps in the context of his discussions with Hume it was important for the latter not to appear too sympathetic to devolution in general or to Unionist formulas for it in particular. Additionally, the SDLP was notably the only party in Strand 1 not to exclude the future involvement in devolution structures of parties linked to violence. This could simply be interpreted as ensuring that down the line, if Hume convinced Adams of the need to compromise, no such hurdle existed for a newly oriented Sinn Fein willing to engage in the political process.

Thus we have the picture of Hume working the Mayhew process

for such gains as might prove possible within it, but keeping one eye on the broader, if then even more problematic, goal of bringing Sinn Fein into the political fold.

The Irish Government

There was one obvious difference between the Irish government delegation and the others: none of the Irish ministers had previous experience of negotiations over the North.

For the Northern parties, there had first been Sunningdale in 1973. The next decade had seen various British-inspired attempts to create internal institutions to promote devolution or dialogue, all fairly miserable failures. And then Brooke had managed to open Strand 1 in 1991. As far as the Northerners were concerned, many of the personnel had been involved in every instance over the years, and were now party leaders or senior figures. Their positions might have been more junior in the earlier events, but the continuity remained clear and strong. A Dublin government had been involved in Sunningdale, but the personnel had of course changed many times over the intervening nineteen years. Something similar could be said of the British government, despite its daily involvement in the direct rule of Northern Ireland since 1974, but there was strong and recent institutional memory of the Brooke talks, both among Conservatives and among the civil servant teams in Belfast and London, when of course the UK had been deeply and directly engaged. The Brooke talks had permitted Dublin engagement only in the *talks about talks*: the wrangling about procedures for the Strand 2 which never opened to permit direct Irish involvement. When Strand 2 finally opened fully, one UUP delegate described them as 'the most ill-prepared group of the Strand 2 lot'.

This lack of direct experience should not be too heavily emphasized: the Irish delegation were, after all, experienced professional politicians of cabinet rank. But certainly there was a sense among everyone present as Strand 2 opened that the Dublin delegates were not prepared for the Unionist onslaught, its ferocity or its longevity. Moreover, they were shocked at the way Unionist negotiators ignored the apparent imbalance in rank between themselves as mere local or regional representatives, comprising at best a few back-bench MPs, and the Irish as executive ministers of a sovereign government. Beyond the purely personal antipathy between Flynn and Paisley, for example, there were initially clashing perceptions of the relationships around the table. Thompson was quickly aware of this:

> I don't think [the Irish delegation] ever recognised the Ulster Unionists or the DUP as equal players in the process. Which made it harder for them to stomach the sort of treatment they were given. They had days of grilling by Paisley and Robinson and others, and it must have been immensely frustrating. Ministers are very busy people, and it's pretty unusual to have a Minister stuck at a table for day after day responding to questions.

This was compounded, in the eyes of Unionists at least, by the lack of cohesion among the coalition partners in the Irish delegation. Paisley hit that particular target quite spectacularly at one early Strand 2 session, when he managed to split O'Malley and Andrews over their parties' clashing expressed positions on the need to alter Articles Two and Three. It was an uneasy coalition in the Dail at that time under Taoiseach Albert Reynolds, between Fianna Fail (including Andrews and Flynn) and their new, junior partners the Progressive Democrats (the PDs, from whom came O'Malley and Wilson). But to demonstrate mixed motives over such a key Unionist issue as the territorial claim to the North was unavoidably to reveal weakness and a lack of cohesion, upon which the Northerners naturally pounced.

Added to such inexperience and internal confusion, was a further contrast between the understandings and strategic vision of the Irish civil servant team, and their ministerial masters. Of the civil servants Dorr, Ó hUiginn and Donoghue, Thompson – himself a civil servant by profession – reflected:

> We'd have meetings with Noel and Sean and David, and you couldn't come out of those meetings without a realisation of the gulf between them and their people at the negotiating table ... They were prominent in the process. Frankly, probably had they been at the table we might have got somewhere. But that's the nature of politics.

All these factors may have both contributed to and flowed from a certain sense of inferiority in Dublin which was still an element of the relationship with Westminster. Since the Anglo-Irish Agreement of 1985, the Irish government had become an official partner with Britain concerning the Northern Ireland issue, but at this stage it was still something of a junior partner in the relationship. It was arguably not until the later 1990s, after many more significant engagements at various levels, and a fundamental realization in London of Dublin's key role in any successful process, that the balance was redressed and the relationship began to operate more closely on a basis of parity. In 1992, even to Stephen in Strand 2, compared to the British the Dublin delegation seemed weak:

> I didn't have the same sort of discussions with the Irish [as with the British], largely because you didn't feel that any one of them could speak for the whole delegation in quite the same way that Mayhew could ... It was pretty clear all through that there was a tension between them, and of course the election proved that to be quite right.

And this insecurity also both explained and manifested itself in the issue of the resumption of Conference meetings in November. Initially suspended until June, both governments were happy to further postpone the scheduled late July meeting into October to permit more talks. But the Irish initially baulked at a further suspension beyond October, in contrast to the British, and eventually insisted on an immovable mid-November compromise. I have referred to the Conference suspension earlier as merely a fig leaf for Unionism, but clearly as time passed it was not without significance to Dublin. The Unionist 'illusion' that the suspensions worked to weaken the Agreement was at least partly shared in Dublin, and the sense of insecurity in both the talks process and the intergovernmental relationship meant that Reynolds insisted that no further suspension could be approved because it would be too great a concession to Unionists. So even symbols could injure Dublin. This was in contrast to the British position on the matter, which was almost neutral and certainly much more relaxed.

What then were the Irish goals for the process? Clearly they were ready to define their satisfaction or otherwise over Strand 1 in parallel with the SDLP: if it pleased Hume, it would please Dublin. As far as Strand 2 was concerned, they knew from the start that their highest card was their agreement to change the constitution by referendum. Fairly soon after the initial prolonged grilling process over opening statements was completed, they defined the price for this in their first paper of the resumed talks in September:

> If ... proposals for constitutional change emerging from the negotiations were to include changes to the Irish Constitution, the strength and quality of the proposed links between both parts of Ireland would be one of the important factors in shaping the judgement of the [Irish] electorate in this regard.

So the concept of cross-border executive power was an Irish goal. Where the Unionist argument said that, in the absence so far of agreement on those structures, the referendum commitment should be given and 'banked' against an eventual overall settlement, Dublin was never of a mind to play that ace before the final hand. Undoubtedly (as was proven in 1998) an agreeable settlement could virtually guarantee a successful referendum on the issue, but the risk of being popularly seen in the Republic to have played the card too early could well have been enough to destabilize the already shaky government coalition. As rumours of ministerial mismanagement circulated in advance of the Beef Tribunal Report, such electoral insecurities could not but impinge on the Irish negotiating position.

But they did continue to explore the possibility of Unionist concessions on the North–South structures as their expressed price for a referendum. And in the closing stages of the talks, as Stephen drew Dublin and the UUP closer through the bilateral and trilateral meetings, the serious engagement demonstrated by both sides bears witness to the genuineness of their enterprise, however distant the goal remained. Nonetheless, the Tribunal sounded the death-knell of both the Southern government and the talks. Once an election was called in the Republic, any further progress was doomed for some time and, in the view of at least Stephen, Mayhew and some of the Northern leaders, doomed for too long a period to be merely suspended. By contrast, the 1996–98 delegation from Dublin, representing Bertie Aherne's much stronger Fianna Fail–PD coalition (and indeed with a now usefully experienced Andrews reinstated as Foreign Minister) demonstrated none of the same insecurities or incoherence.

Often in Anglo-Irish politics, Dublin has been seen as, and has acted as, the sponsor of Northern nationalism. Tempered only by the abiding role of Hume, in return, as a key adviser to Dublin through countless Irish administrations, this sponsorship role has become a given, certainly with some reason. And the comparison has often been drawn between this and the much more fractious relationship between London and Unionism. Clearly happy to be guided by the SDLP for the most part in Strand 1 matters, and certainly also advised and influenced by Hume and his party in other Strands, the Irish delegation and government did indeed look out for SDLP interests in general. An obvious mix of despondency and cynicism set in rapidly among Andrews and his colleagues when DUP antics raised temperatures and rendered proceedings close to farce. This became very clear on the first day back in September, when the table was virtually deluged with pieces of paper representing the multiple unnumbered, unprioritized and unauthored Strand 2 agenda suggestions. That very evening, Reynolds and the delegation met with Hume and his lieutenants to tell them that, in the Dublin view, the talks were going to founder over Unionist rejection of the SDLP panel in Strand 1 within a month, as the Conference meeting loomed. The logical reaction, they advised their Northern colleagues, was to plot a soft landing for themselves in advance of the inevitable breakdown of talks.

Even though the spark of Irish belief was perhaps rekindled during those three late-stage October meetings with the UUP, the pending election made it a moot point. By the time of that abrupt conclusion, the Dublin delegation had managed to maintain their own cards largely in their hand, had gained great insight into the UUP position and had perhaps prised out the possibility of a little Unionist movement on that position, but had made little substantive gain in negotiating terms. Perhaps overall, their most significant result, symbolic and yet vital, was to have engaged Northern Unionism in direct negotiation for the first time in 19 years; and to have enticed some, if not all, Unionist negotiators to Dublin, in a novel if implicit recognition of the Republic's right to involvement and its central importance in the dynamics of the

conflict. But there was general consensus among the other participants that the Dublin negotiators served a painful but necessary
apprenticeship which could only bear fruit in the future.

The British Government

By and large, the British government tended to view itself as the
prime mover in the entire process. A degree of this was to be
expected, given that the UK has a proprietary role towards the part
of its domestic territory designated Northern Ireland. Moreover,
this role of director of proceedings had been well entrenched over
many years of British government dealings with the parties and
personalities of Northern politics. Additionally, insofar as the whole
negotiating initiative had begun with Peter Brooke, there is an
arguable British claim to ownership. It was British Secretary of State
Brooke who made the initial advances to the Northern parties in
1989, who managed the shuttle-mediation for the subsequent 18
months of talks about talks, and who chaired the 1991 Strand 1
talks.

Mayhew assumed Brooke's mantle in April 1992 with a self-
assured manner that reflected a conviction that he was very
definitely in control. His so-called 'patrician' manner tended only
to reinforce the impression, although this is not to contradict in
any way the comments of many participants who found him
personally amiable – 'a delightful person, very charming, easy to get
on with', as Stephen described him – and professionally intelligent
and skilled. Mayhew demonstrated a geniality and bonhomie
which was attractive to many. And yet, as the 'Ninian Stephen
document' (Appendix 2) demonstrates all too clearly, there was
immense British pressure (and strangely insistent optimism, born
mostly out of desperation) in the closing days of October.

In any case, the British government and delegation in all the
events concerning the negotiations certainly acted on the assumption that they were in control. This was undoubtedly manifest in
the London–Dublin relationship. It was not yet, after six years of its
post-Agreement context, a partnership of anything approaching
equals. And, as I suggested earlier, part of this dynamic was a
continuous underestimation of the necessity and importance of
Dublin's contribution to any overall solution. This latter view

encouraged Britain to downplay not only Dublin's share in the responsibilities of any final settlement, but also its participation in the process of reaching that settlement. The Irish delegation themselves blunted the effect of this high-handedness in turn by being a little under par in experience, robustness and cohesion. The relationship of the governments did lead to tensions on occasion, as when the Irish insecurity over continued postponements of the Conference meeting was met by British incomprehension in October.

When it came to the Northern parties, most of the key individuals in the Northern delegations, among them Hume, Molyneaux, Paisley, Maginnis, and Mallon, were backbenchers in the government of which the British delegation were ministers. This served only to increase the proprietor's attitude to Northern Ireland and all within it. In the talks, this manifested itself not in any bullying or disrespect, but there was a sense in which Britain often tried to set the agenda, to push past obstacles, to apply pressure. This was perhaps very understandable in Strand 1, where Mayhew was in the chair. But it spilled over substantially into Strand 2 as well. Thompson cites one reason why there may have been more urgency on the British side:

> I'm absolutely convinced that Mayhew wanted to be the Northern Ireland Secretary who pulled off a solution. There's no question about that ... the British were almost desperate to get an agreement out of the process.

So there were, in other words, both personal and political/professional imperatives behind the British approach.

However, the complexity of the British role must be acknowledged. In Brooke's Strand 1, I described him as 'simultaneously attempting both to be the neutral referee and to hold office as the most powerful player in the game' (Bloomfield, 1997, p. 165). Indeed, an earlier incumbent, Jim Prior, described the entire role of the Secretary in contradictory terms:

> As Secretary of State for Northern Ireland I found myself performing a dual role, as a Governor-General representing the Queen and as such the enemy of every Republican in the

province, but also ... acting like a referee in a boxing ring whose authority seemed to be resented equally by both sides. I was combining two tasks kept separate until the introduction of direct rule. (Prior, 1986, pp. 181–2)

Mayhew himself recognized the complexities of his dual role in his opening presentation to Strand 2:

I enter Strand 2 as a participant rather than as Chairman. Yet it continues to be as important to me to facilitate agreement as to argue my own corner.

So he described himself as a facilitatory chair of Strand 1 who conducted the meetings, not perhaps engaging in the debate so much as setting and monitoring the parameters in which it was held. Nonetheless, it was Mayhew who largely drove the Strand 1 agenda by offering discussion papers to guide and develop dialogue, especially in the early stages. It was Strand 2 where the role became much more literally that of referee and player. It was also something of a minefield for the British: the Unionists, particularly Paisley's delegation, believed that Britain should be much more assertive and partial against the Irish position, defending Northern Ireland's constitutional position against the Irish territorial claim, and in general safeguarding British sovereignty in Northern Ireland. Even in Strand 1, Paisley had tried to push Mayhew to take a stand over the devolution formulas, to express the British preference. Mayhew dealt with the demand diplomatically, asserting that his definition of an acceptable formula was largely one which would satisfy the four Northern parties, but accepting also that such a formula was likely to be close to the Unionist proposals. In Strand 2, he was much more resistant to Unionist pressure so that, while he did exert some energy in keeping the Government of Ireland Act (the British legislation which the Irish saw as the rough equivalent of their own Articles Two and Three) off the agenda, he tried to avoid taking positions which might later be quoted supportively by Unionists. Anything which might upset the working relationship between him and his Irish counterparts was avoided, despite the DUP tactic of trying to drive wedges between every possible coalition permutation around the table. When it came to the small number of Strand 3 meetings, Unionist pressure was at its highest on Mayhew to take a fully confrontational role against the Irish, and to negotiate in defence of Northern Ireland. But the wider relationship of co-operation between the two governments was always going to outweigh such tensions, and Mayhew effectively resisted Paisley's best attempts.

Mayhew and his team did not act as sponsors of Unionism in the way that Dublin sponsored, and worked very closely with, the SDLP. At the very least, there was always a residual tension between the Unionists and Britain, and their suspicions of British motives were never put to rest. This was, after all, the British government which had gone over their heads to deal with Dublin and produce the hated Anglo-Irish Agreement. But Mayhew certainly had both a sympathy for the Unionists' position, and an understanding of where they would and would not make concessions. He told the Irish, informally but emphatically, that the Unionists would never accept the SDLP Panel proposal, and they believed his insight. So while hardly a close ally of Unionism in many respects, and indeed a leading light in a process that clearly demanded change from them, Mayhew had empathy for, and insight into, their views which helped set the parameters of dialogue, and was of some useful reassurance around the table.

For the prolonged duration of Thatcher's, and then Major's, Conservative government – thirteen years and counting at the time of the talks – it is easy to see British policy on Northern Ireland as primarily security-oriented. (Indeed, this helps in part to explain the subsequent lack of political generosity shown by Major and Mayhew towards Republicanism after the 1994 IRA ceasefire: having gained a security coup, some of the steam immediately seemed to go out of British efforts to make further progress.) With hindsight, knowing that at another very unofficial level Mayhew was in busy dialogue with Sinn Fein over the possibilities of an IRA ceasefire, one can posit an interpretation of British strategy as seeking the formula for political settlement – or at least some substantive political progress, such as a Heads of Agreement for future attention – in the talks while chasing a security settlement through the clandestine communication channel. Mayhew demonstrated an eagerness to press forward on both these fronts which belied the difficulties of the tasks involved. In Thompson's words, he was 'desperate' for a settlement. Not only would it have constituted progress in the dual dialogue in which Britain was engaged. Of course, it would also have played domestically in Britain as a dramatic coup for Mayhew and the government. Major was naturally enthused by this possibility: with a dwindling majority, his government sorely needed the eclat which would accompany such a political success.

British goals, like those of most participants, were frustrated by the inconclusive collapse of the talks. But, despite the reality that it was the Irish delegation's domestic troubles which actually signalled the end of the negotiations, it is fair to say that Britain's goals for the talks were blocked not by any obvious mistakes by Mayhew so much as by an over-enthusiasm on his part, which occasionally proved annoying to others, and by a degree of intransigence among the Northern political parties, and the Unionists in particular. One British gain of some significance was that, following these talks, the intergovernment relationship was deepened and strengthened, simply by the ingraining of the closer cooperative activity demanded by the talks.

The two governments

This partnership between Ireland and the UK brought its own dynamic to the process. As the overall sponsors of negotiation, the governments acted as the driving force of the talks. Certainly they did not approach the arrangements of the 1996–98 talks, where chair George Mitchell frequently admitted that the two governments – indeed the two prime ministers – were the 'engine-room' for the talks process, largely controlling the dynamic while Mitchell remained the titular director. In stark comparison, Stephen was much less constrained:

> With Mayhew, I discussed from time to time how we might advance matters. From time to time there seemed to be a breakdown imminent, and we would talk about what we could do to overcome it. I didn't have the same discussions with the Irish.

Such discussions 'from time to time' were much less directive than in the later process. And indeed, Stephen's lack of political clout outside the negotiating room was very different from that of Mitchell who, for all his individual impartiality, was clearly carrying at all times some degree of White House authority which demanded respect and response:

> My function was a very limited one, namely not for a moment to arbitrate or mediate, but simply to make possible the proceedings by being a completely neutral chairman ... I didn't have any commitment: I didn't go there with anything to lose if it failed or to gain if it succeeded. (Stephen)

Having such a 'neutral' role made Stephen much less of any threat to the parties involved, including the governments who, at the higher level, still clearly controlled the parameters of dialogue through their joint design of the talks and their dictation of Conference dates. But for all their coherence and partnership at that overall, intergovernmental level, the relationship was less close in the talks than might have been supposed. Between the two civil servant teams, for example, Thompson recalls,

> There wasn't as close contact as you might have expected. I would always have seen each of them separately, and I think they operated pretty much as separate units ... Obviously they normally had quite close communication in the context of the Agreement and those regular meetings, but all of that was very deliberately put into abeyance to accommodate the Unionists. So it may be that during the talks period there was rather less communication between the two. At least I wasn't aware of frequent or constant communication between the two.

This was in direct contrast to the close teamwork between civil servants from 1994 onwards, when they were frequently and deeply involved in jointly negotiating forms of words for key documents to reflect developments in the wider peace process. For Thompson, indeed, the two governments might, in the later stages, have played more of a driving role:

> In a sense [the governments] were the engine room of most of the ideas and proposals that were put on the table. But they were

very, very reluctant to be the driving force of the process, and never at any stage let themselves move into that role. In fact, towards the end of the process, Sir Ninian issued a mild rebuke to the two governments, for failing to provide enough impetus to the process through the Strand 3 side of it. We did feel at that stage that with a bit more push from the two most powerful players, some compromise might have been reached which could then have led to other compromises which might have enabled the sketching out of a skeleton agreement.

For each delegation, then, there were moments of gain, of learning, of new understandings and of progress, but also, ultimately, of frustration and failure. As each party considered or at least glimpsed the possibilities of gains and concessions, they permanently increased the overall degree of understanding and acknowledgement of the shape of an eventual settlement. While nothing was signed up to, many of the substantial implications of such a settlement were at the very least considered, designed and clarified. The 1998 Good Friday Agreement contains very significant amounts of what was discussed in 1992, and the Mayhew talks thus demand to be seen as a vital, if only partial, step towards that success. A year previously, there had been serious doubts expressed as to each of the Northern parties' political will and commitment to the dialogue process. This time around, by contrast, all of them – including even the DUP, if only in an early Strand 1 stage – demonstrated a sense of engagement and serious commitment, which, if it left them still short of success, nevertheless moved the wave further up the beach.

10
Conclusion: Developing Dialogue: 'Stockpiling Obstacles'

I chose the title of this work carefully: despite some early expectations among participants and the occasional genuine, but limited,
breakthrough, the Mayhew talks never truly looked like reaching a
settlement. It is much more realistic to see the process as one of
building on the previous year's effort towards developing the
process of dialogue. Peter Brooke offered an image to represent this
approach:

> What you are looking at in Northern Ireland in terms of these
> negotiations are a series of waves advancing up the beach. And
> the important thing is that one day the wave will reach the top
> of the beach and you will have achieved your objective. Every
> wave should get further than the last one, in other words you
> continue to advance but you must be patient and not frustrated
> if particular waves are not strong enough to get there.
> (Bloomfield, 1997, p. 144)

The metaphor is apt, implying a certain inevitability of gradual, if
uneven, progress by stages. While he didn't necessarily foresee a
complete settlement as feasible in one attempt, he believed his job
was to push the wave further up the beach, so that the next might
flow still further up. It is in such a developmental light that both
the Brooke and the Mayhew talks can be seen as vital precursors of
the subsequent talks which led to the much more significant wave
that became the Good Friday Agreement. Likewise, in his latter
desperation to reach some kind of outcome, even if only a Heads of

Agreement, Mayhew was also working with an eye to the future in his aim of establishing a launching point for a restart.

So further developmental work under Mayhew and especially Stephen served to build on Brooke's beginnings, to push the door a little further open and to make sure it remained open for future attempts. In Stephen's words, this went some way to explain the minimalist nature of the final agreed statement:

> We thought that [talks] would be resumed. And therefore there was a strong feeling that very little should be said, because anything that might be said would be so easily turned into a stumbling block on resumption.

Among Northern participants, perhaps only Hume shared this outlook. In his ongoing discussions with Adams, he was already painting on a broader canvas, while Alliance and most of the Unionists felt merely disappointment and frustration at the collapse of talks, rather than any sense of potential for future development. But this was certainly the overview shared by both governments, and by Stephen, as is demonstrated in the letter they sent to him following the conclusion of the talks:

> We consider that the dialogue which has taken place hitherto has been valuable, and that further dialogue is both necessary and desirable ... If agreement is reached on the basis of future talks, we hope it might be possible to call once more on your services.

The facilitator's role

Even allowing for his own modesty, Stephen played a modest if appropriate role. By his own admission, he had no stake whatsoever in the substantive outcome of talks. One can assume, naturally, that there was a desire to produce a result which would do credit to Stephen and also to Australia; but such success would have had little to do with the shape of any settlement: simply producing agreement – any agreement endorsed by all delegations – would have satisfied this desire. Neither Stephen nor Australia had any particular interest in the actualities of Northern Irish (or Irish) politics.

By that fact alone, Stephen qualifies as a facilitator, one oriented totally towards managing a process within which the other actors might or might not fashion a successful agreement over the content of the talks. As he remarks disarmingly, 'I had no concept of promoting a deal, very largely because I had no idea what that deal should be. I was simply to preside over them, and get them talking together.' Stephen himself will admit to some childhood holiday visits to Ireland, and an early education in Britain before moving to Australia in his teens, 'but I had no views one way or the other'. Nonetheless, his previous professional life, as an Australian diplomat within the British Commonwealth, furnished him with a closer initial empathy for Britain than for Ireland. Of course he could not help but have his own opinions about some of the issues which might contribute to a deal:

> I had a good deal of sympathy for the Unionists on the question of the Irish constitution. [Articles Two and Three] did seem to me a highly provocative statement which de Valera had included in the constitution ... It did seem a pretty essential feature that the Irish should abandon that.

And further, his understanding of his brief included simply the proviso that 'Ulster was to remain within Britain, but otherwise matters were very fluid'.

But his skill in the facilitator's role effectively prevented his opinions on substantive matters from getting in the way of his even-handedness, and other participants' glowing comments about his performance ('the real hero of the piece', as one Unionist delegate called him) reflect this. Indeed, Stephen and Thompson may be the only individuals to emerge from the talks without a single critical barb directed toward them. However, it could be added that this benign attitude toward Stephen was also encouraged by that precise element which gave him legitimacy in his role: his remoteness from the substance of the conflict removed from him any threat to the participants. While it in one sense disempowered him – he was completely powerless to punish or sanction, to bribe or reward, outside the negotiating room and in the political world of Anglo-Irish politics – it simultaneously rendered him acceptable as sufficiently impartial to exercise his chair's authority fairly to all. He could be trusted; he did not need to be feared.

He was, thus, the antithesis of a participant. For Stephen, there were none of the complications or contradictions of role that Mayhew had. He was not a player in the game, nor was he in any sense a referee, for he had no punitive sanction to impose on anyone, even to exclude them in any way from his process:

> I didn't do anything, except just sit there ... I controlled the process to the extent that I reflected the wishes of the various people taking part in the process. They said, 'This is what we'd like to do,' and I said 'Okay, let's do it.'

This is rather too self-effacing. Stephen also admits that the two non-negotiating days of most weeks were intensely busy for him and Thompson: 'thinking of proposals, procedures to be adopted. We continually pushed in that sense.' But the sense of which he speaks was a strictly procedural one. Neither Stephen nor his assistant were engaged in designing solutions to issues on the table, tempting though it might have been during the more frustrating sessions. But they joked about it, nonetheless:

> I kept saying, to George [Thompson] and to my wife during it all, 'If only we could be given a few weeks to write out a solution.' Then we could have gone to each of the parties and said, 'Tell us what's wrong with this, why the interests of the people you speak for are really adversely affected by this.' ... And then we'd work our way to an agreement. But I knew all along that that was quite unrealistic. (Stephen)

And there were times, Thompson recalls, when the parties might have been happy for the facilitators to engage in the substantive issues:

> There was a surprising amount of freedom. We were taken aback at the extent to which the parties did defer to Sir Ninian to offer suggestions about everything from procedural to substantive matters ... That said, we rarely took a step on procedural matters without first consulting all of the parties to the talks: agenda-setting, for example. For procedure, we consulted and then when

we were fairly confident that we would have general agreement, we put something on the table.

Thus, whatever his own opinions, and even despite encouragement from the delegations, the Australian facilitator was scrupulous in his refusal to engage substantively, avoiding expressions of partiality or self-interest. It is a considerable tribute to him and to his assistant that they seem never to have deviated from this strict interpretation of their role, while yet making significant strides in moving the process along and in deepening the quality of the engagement. Even as pressure mounted in October, they responded carefully to Mayhew's Heads of Agreement plan. While they did happily accept the reorienting of the agenda across the three Strands, fitting it in effectively with their own move to bilateral discussions, they resolutely refused his offer to 'ghost-write' the amalgamated report (see Appendix 2). And, in terms of moving waves up the beach, Stephen attended dutifully to promoting his wave as far as possible, even though it might not have become really evident until the arrival of George Mitchell's tidal wave.

The talks structure

The structure of the negotiations – the design and arrangement of the process – was largely inherited intact from Brooke, since it was still based completely on Brooke's precise formula. The three-stranded structure, the banking principle, the geographical and physical arrangements, the delegation size, the role – and even the identity – of the Strand 2 chair, the content of the Strand 1 agenda: these and many other aspects were all taken as read in April 1992.

What was different from the previous attempt, however, was the effective use of non-plenary sessions. There had been some small degree of committee work under Brooke, and some minor element of 'corridoring', that is, unofficial discussions outside the formal negotiating process. But these options were pursued with much more emphasis right from the start of the 1992 process. The Strand 1 participants quickly and readily established several sub-committees, the most important being the Structures Sub-Committee which considered the devolution proposals and eventually came close to agreement over the *Possible Outline Framework* paper. And the plenary was happy to extend the life and work of the Sub-Committee on a repeated basis. The most dramatic instance of Strand 1 corridoring was the spontaneous outburst of informal bilateral discussion on Friday 29 May, which caused Jeremy Hanley, the day's chair, to postpone his departure several times. In the space of two and a half hours, these meetings produced a rapid series of drafts of an agreed Sub-Committee report analysing the current impasse and proposing a path through it. It was this report which enabled the much deeper and substantive negotiation which led directly to the *Possible Outline Framework* of 3–10 June. The lesson had been learnt the previous year that the formal plenary was rarely the place to reach beyond rhetoric into real negotiation.

However, when Strand 2 opened, new insecurities faced all the participants, with a new agenda and an additional delegation. This is the likeliest explanation for the fact that, while the sub-committee system was enthusiastically implemented, it was simultaneously circumscribed by the fact that on all sides too many of the key plenary figures simply nominated themselves onto the Sub-Committee. The effect was that it functioned partly as a plenary in miniature. This was much more marked than in the key Strand 1 Structures Sub-Committee, for example, where no leaders participated in the three-person delegations. 'Right from the outset,' remarked Thompson, 'the [Strand 2] committee was far too unwieldy.' This led to some rather surreal situations where almost the identical group of people would prepare a sub-committee report, and then convene themselves as the plenary to adopt the report. Clearly, a further deconstruction of the rather starched and formal plenary interaction was needed. 'We did on occasion,' noted Thompson, 'have what we called drafting groups, which were more productive, where we'd have just one or two representatives from each team, where we were trying to thrash out draft reports from the committee to plenary, and that sort of thing.' But a still greater degree of informality was required. This arrived in the form of unminuted bilaterals, which Stephen introduced in the final weeks of Strand 2:

As far as negotiation was concerned, the interesting thing really was how impossible it would have been around the big table to have one party making a proposal and another listening and responding in any helpful way. Whereas to have one party in the room talking to us, and then our walking down the corridor to the other party to say, 'Look at this: what's your reaction?' really worked very well. The difference was quite extraordinary. It really began with the journeying from one party to another down the corridor on the part of George.

Thompson agrees on the positive nature of the bilaterals: 'We found those meetings much more productive, and there was a genuine willingness on the part of all the parties to find a way forward.'

In contrast to the Brooke talks of the previous year, for large periods of Stephen's negotiations the plenary became the exception, and the sub-committee the rule. But the 'corridoring' of the previous year was also expanded, if not sufficiently:

> It happened more towards the end. It wasn't too late, but there wasn't enough of it ... There was lots of opportunity for corridor discussions at morning and afternoon teabreaks. (Except for the DUP, who didn't associate with the others much at all. Paisley's group would not eat with the others; his group ate in a separate dining-room.) ... You would often get chats between the SDLP and the Ulster Unionists ... The Alliance also had good relations with the SDLP and the UUP. (Stephen)

With the immense benefit of hindsight, it is easy to characterize the talks, particularly in Strand 2, as limping through from one crisis to the next, failing to resolve the substance of the last crisis, but rather carrying it forward into the next. For Thompson, this was at least partially a flaw of the inherited three-strand process and especially the banking principle. While the design was intended to facilitate addressing all aspects without having to reach full agreement on one before moving to another, and while this was a worthy goal, in fact the result was rather less positive:

> The three-stranded process, the 'Riddle of the Strands', was perhaps a little too unwieldy. It did conveniently identify the different aspects or dimensions of the problem. But it was always going to be difficult to keep those balls in the air simultaneously, and it had proved impossible to reach agreement on one before moving on to another.

What we tended to do in the process was we'd come up against an obstacle, and we'd set it aside and move on to the next challenge. We'd meet an obstacle, we'd say, 'Let's not let that bring the whole thing down, let's park that, and we'll move on to the next.' Always in the hope that in the discussion of the next agenda item or the next issue, there would be a greater sense of co-operation and commonality among the parties which might then improve the prospects of revisiting obstacles that held up progress. But instead all we were doing was building up a backlog of obstacles that we never really got over. Yes, we were stockpiling obstacles. (Thompson)

Yet within and around that process, there were also real, if occasional, moments of progress. For example:

We were probably at our most pessimistic just prior to the Dublin meeting. But the Dublin meeting was a good one; we felt that real progress had been made ... There had been some rather important breakthroughs. That was where the Irish agreed that they could – not would – sponsor a referendum to change Articles Two and Three of the constitution ... We had a lot of argument over substituting 'would' for 'could', but nevertheless the UUP agreed that it was progress, and that it was sufficient basis on which to continue talking. (Thompson)

Thompson does not go on to say that this progress coincided with the DUP absence from the table, but it may be assumed that this was a factor which both cooled the temperature around the table and also freed the UUP from having to look too often over their shoulders to watch their Unionist rivals. However, there was frustration for the facilitators just at this encouraging point. An obstacle suddenly appeared from far outside the negotiating environment which effectively and totally disabled one key delegation:

We did feel that we might have got to the stage where we could have got the Irish to sign on to a form of wording to sponsor a referendum. We were very close to that point, but all hope evaporated as the [Irish] election drew closer. The concession over Articles Two and Three was often tantalisingly close. I always felt that, if the Irish government were prepared to move from 'could' to 'would', that could act as a circuit-breaker for getting concessions from the UUP about the nature of the North–South structures. I felt they were often almost on the point of being prepared to sign on to that form of words. But certainly not ahead of an election. But had they been re-elected, and had the Unionists got over a meeting of the Anglo-Irish Conference, then we could have resumed and continued to make progress. (Thompson)

Within the dialogue process, as inherited from Brooke and with only minor variations, Strand 2 represented a modestly effective mediation and a useful structure, which included a shift towards smaller-scale, more focused interactions. It might have produced at least an initial result (such as a deal over Articles Two and Three and the executive power of North–South institutions), but outside events meant that it did not have the necessary time.

Moments of interest

Finally, for all the overall failure of the talks, there were several key moments during the process, the examination of which can help us both to see those gains which were made in a more positive light, as well as perhaps to understand better why more progress was not made.

Common Principles, 6 May

Although hardly surrounded by much drama, the production of the *Common Principles* document was a small, straightforward but significant moment. On only the third negotiating day of Strand 1, and in the space of just one day, 16 governing principles for devolution structures were debated and agreed. The significance of the moment lies first in the fact that it was the first agreement reached, and that it was done with little rancour. This was an encouraging sign of co-operative discussion, reinforcing the perceptions that participants were building on the 'chemistry' of the previous year, and that the political will existed among all four parties to address themselves seriously to the goal of making progress. Secondly, the principles themselves served not only as a framework for analysing and assessing subsequent devolution proposals, for example during the 13 May discussions of the four models for power-sharing government. They were also extrapolated more than once as principles which could also be applied in Strand 2: on 10 September, the day following the DUP's withdrawal from active engagement, the remaining parties used the Strand 1 template to agree a set of principles to be applied similarly to any Strand 2 structures. Overall, the document demonstrated that, whatever differences existed, there was at least a broad consensus on the initial definitions of a democratic Northern Ireland.

Corridoring, 29 May

The apparently spontaneous round of unofficial talks on Friday 29 May was an interesting, and as yet not fully explained, phenomenon. The previous days had bogged down deeply in the Sub-Committee, as each party defended its own paper on what was preventing progress in their efforts, and attacked all the other party papers. For good measure in the course of these protectionist arguments, Robinson of the DUP had raised the old spectre of 'other documents', in which Peter Brooke had allegedly provided extra written assurances in a letter to the two Unionist leaders beyond his agreed March 1991 formula for talks. (It had been a stale argument long before this, and although the truth of the situation is still unknown, it is likely that such a letter did exist but that it did little more than reinforce in Unionist-friendly terms the agreed condition that the Government of Ireland Act and the constitutional status of Northern Ireland within the UK were not negotiable during the talks.) This served to sour the atmosphere further, and the concerted efforts of David Fell, in the Sub-Committee chair on the Friday morning, failed to improve matters. However, clearly Robinson, Empey, Fell and Farren among others were actively engaged in trying to move the discussion on to more positive ground. Hanley, back in the chair by the afternoon, adjourned the session for the day at 4pm, and delegates walked the corridors and returned to their party offices. It was now that the conversations continued in more direct fashion as individuals talked to each other, and as messages began to circulate around the corridors. Hanley postponed his departure twice, and by 6.30pm that evening, an all-party draft of a strategy for progress was in place. This led, in turn, to further redrafting activities over the ensuing weekend. The report finally presented to Monday's plenary dislodged the blockage and from then on the Sub-Committee seemed to operate in a much more proactive fashion. The pace of exchange picked up dramatically, and interaction was intense enough for Robinson and his delegation to threaten a walk-out during the afternoon. But by 11.30 that night they had produced a promising draft of the *Possible Outline Framework*.

As yet, no participant or analyst has explained exactly why this unofficial negotiation broke out at this stage. Perhaps it was simply a degree of serendipity surrounding the positive efforts of those individuals mentioned earlier: Empey, Robinson and Farren could all be characterized as, relatively speaking at least within their own parties, moderates of some standing. At this fairly early stage, the DUP had not yet dismissed the entire process and, in the course of testing out the potential of Strand 1 to produce a DUP-friendly result, Robinson was still actively engaged in seeking progress. He and Empey drove the dramatically reinvigorated discussions of the following week, with support from Farren and Durkan, towards a formula for devolution which, at midnight on 3 June, looked briefly like an agreed solution.

If we cannot fully explain the occurrence, we can at least examine its effect. Initially, of course, it led to the generation of optimism and enthusiasm: the delegations came close to a core agreement on their central agenda. But subsequently, its failure generated an even stronger sense of despair, as the parties then indulged in blaming each other for its failure. In particular, Unionists took from this a deep sense of grievance that the SDLP alone – or indeed John Hume himself – had consciously backed away from genuine success in Strand 1 by reinserting and insisting upon the wholly unacceptable Panel ingredient. Fair or otherwise, that perception stayed with them, and as the talks finally ended five months later it became Unionist orthodoxy to trace the downfall at least partly to this specific failure of the SDLP.

The Possible Outline Framework, 3 June

This document represented the high-point of Strand 1 efforts. Following the breaking of the log-jam after the corridoring success at the end of May, the Structures Sub-Committee went into the highest gear it achieved. Driven by able party lieutenants like Empey, Durkan and Robinson, they spent a long day on 1 June, splitting into two sub-groups to speed the process, drawing closer on the possibilities of a devolution structure. By late on Tuesday night, this had become a draft of the *Possible Outline Framework (to assist discussion)*, and by the early hours of Thursday morning it had been initialled by members of all four parties. The late-night drama of this breakthrough moment was dispelled, at least according to the Unionist canon, by Hume's angry refusal to endorse the formula overnight.

Even eight years later, there remains some confusion about these events, and participants still retain a degree of reticence, especially on the SDLP side. What is beyond doubt is that the *Possible Outline Framework* was going through a fierce redrafting process: towards the climax, drafts were going out of date every 30 minutes. What also seems fairly certain is that at least one set of SDLP initials went on to the final 12.45am draft, alongside those of other parties. And finally, Hume rejected the document as soon as he himself saw it. Beyond these bare facts, I can unfortunately offer only the colourful, if somewhat slanted, detail provided by a DUP delegate (see Chapter 9). It seems clear that Durkan and Hume exchanged some heated words over the initialling of the *Framework*. This may be a somewhat partisan and simplistic version of events, but undoubtedly Sub-Committee members of all four parties did initial a devolution formula based upon the *Framework* that night. And yet within a week it had been reduced to a series of constituent parts of a formula, significant elements of which the SDLP refused to endorse subject to development in Strand 2. Hume's party must certainly bear the responsibility for this volte-face, even if the Unionist explanation of nationalist perfidy is a little too simple to account for the whole dynamic.

But although the SDLP rowed back from their initial acceptance, the text changed little over the following week, alterations in the main consisting of the insertion of the SDLP's reservations at various points. The full text of the 10 June *Framework*, including the SDLP reservations, is offered in Appendix 1. Long after the collapse of the Mayhew talks, the participants retained the memory along with the realization that any ultimately successful Strand 1 outcome was unlikely to be far away from the gist of the *Framework*.

(And so events proved in 1998.) Another wave had established a new high point on the beach, even if it washed back down again with great rapidity.

Interestingly, Mayhew was largely uninvolved in the main sessions leading up to this point, since he was not a delegate to the Sub-Committee. Instead, David Fell and Jeremy Hanley took the chair for most of the time. But few participants recall any great act of facilitation on the part of either chair. Rather, the sense was of delegates themselves acting in concert and taking control of the proceedings – a pattern that emerged during the corridoring interval and which developed from there. Alliance Deputy Leader Seamus Close recalled,

> There was a fair degree of dialogue in the committee. There was a genuine dialogue there, when we worked into the early hours of the morning, that led up to the understandings of 10 June.

What is most interesting here is that the clearest memories are of delegates themselves suddenly getting serious and moving past the rhetoric. The incident – which in one sense came so near and yet so far – should have encouraged delegates in their own abilities and negotiating skills. More importantly, on a broader level, the event calls into question the popular view that there was a lack of political will in the delegations to take the talks anywhere positive.

Mayhew's 1 July Statement

By late June, the pressure from Dublin and the SDLP was intense regarding the urgency of opening Strand 2. Paisley was still holding out strongly against the idea, and his party had already reached its post-*Framework* decision that the talks would go nowhere good and so should be prevented from going anywhere too dangerous. In turn, general exasperation at the DUP's obstructionism was mounting on all sides. Both Paisley and the UUP were pressing Mayhew to pronounce on the British preference for Strand 1 structures (on the accurate assumption, of course, that he would endorse their proposed version, and then virtually enforce agreement on it). Mayhew, supported by Hume, was having nothing to do with the idea, although he recognised that perhaps some nod towards the viability of their *Framework* model might win some concession in return. Additionally, they had also been pushing him to adopt an explicit British stance opposed to Articles Two and Three. Again, he resisted this while turning it to use as he drafted his statement. Throughout the 1 July negotiations, Mayhew played an effective if delicate game of both indulging and overruling Unionist feelings. The statement of intent to open Strand 2 which he finally tabled in the plenary was an impressive feat of drafting. It met some of their demands and at least addressed and acknowledged all their fears efficiently enough to finally remove or neutralize all their objections. Thus was Strand 2 opened.

Thursday 3 September

By all accounts, this day was one of the lowest of the process. And its events had serious negative implications for what followed. This was during the first few days of the post-summer restart of Strand 2 when, to the amusement of the reader but to the exasperation of those involved, the Strand 2 Committee tried to agree on the agenda for their discussions. In particular, their task of the day was to agree the agenda of sub-items under Item 6 (*Fundamental Aspects of the Problem: underlying realities; identity; allegiance; constitutional issues*). After a troublesome and tetchy Wednesday session, Stephen opened Thursday's business by suggesting the delegations outline their view of the obstacles to Strand 2 progress. The result was a collection of fairly angry, partisan, blame-placing documents. But from the papers, Stephen drew up a composite list of agenda items concerning obstacles to progress, logically placing the most frequently mentioned items at the top of the agenda. The initial argument then broke out, Dublin demanding that Articles Two and Three be moved down the agenda, while the DUP argued for their placement at the top. Eventually, after a flurry of separate unheaded and unnumbered versions of the agenda, Stephen drew up a final agenda and forced a vote. An angry DUP delegation voted against, but were alone in doing so. There was an outburst of Paisley's rage, when he demanded a recess and then complained bitterly that the Chair was moving outside the Strand 2 remit by accepting Britain's Government of Ireland Act as a topic for debate.

It was the first truly bad-tempered day of Strand 2 (but by no means the last). But, for better or worse, it clearly affected two delegations in particular. First, the DUP let their feelings be known in no uncertain way, and began to threaten a boycott of Strand 2. It is very possible that this was the day when the party took the decision, conscious or otherwise, that they were not going to go to Dublin, that their only interest in Strand 2 was to attack Dublin over the Articles, and that there might be nothing in these talks for them.

Second, their performance clearly had a serious effect on Dublin's optimism levels. Having watched the DUP antics in full display for the first time, it is no surprise that by the evening the Irish delegation were warning the SDLP that Unionist intransigence would ensure that the talks failed and so the best strategy was to avoid blame for the inevitable collapse. Obviously, from this moment onward with only a few flickers of indication otherwise, the Irish government began to lose serious faith in the process. It was not a happy day, for the parties or the process, but it was nevertheless an important one in shifting and reducing the commitment and expectations of at least two of the parties.

The move to Dublin

Only three days of official plenary talks took place in Dublin, 21–23 September. But it was nonetheless an immensely significant event. First, there was great significance, symbolic and real, in the arrival of the UUP in the Republic's capital for official negotiations with the Irish government. It was a small but important coup for the Irish, a moment of perhaps shaky pride for the UUP (who continually insisted they were happy to preach the gospel of Unionism wherever they found themselves), and a moment of flustered embarrassment and anger for the DUP.

Second, there was also significance in the DUP's absence. The timing of events permits no other explanation than that Paisley carefully manufactured the argument over the place of Articles Two and Three on the agenda to serve the twin aims of disrupting the process and providing an excuse to avoid a DUP foray into the enemy's capital. The McCrea faction in the DUP would never have stomached such an appearance in Dublin Castle. No one was sure of the DUP's intentions until almost the last moment: Stephen thought Paisley would go; Thompson was certain he wouldn't. But Paisley orchestrated events to the extent that he got a lot of coverage for his anti-Dublin views, which would serve him well with his own hardliners, even if it brought him the opprobrium of almost everyone else.

Third, however, the DUP's absence brought opportunities for progress to others. The temperature around the table lowered, and it was possible for the Irish and the UUP to begin to interact in a more meaningful way. Thompson certainly saw progress, even if he hadn't expected it:

> We were probably at our most pessimistic just prior to the Dublin meeting. But ... we felt that real progress had been made at the Dublin meeting ... There had been some rather important breakthroughs. That was where the Irish agreed [...] they could sponsor a referendum.

While nothing specific in the Dublin conversations proves it, it is reasonable to assume that this drawing closer of the Irish and the UUP was a necessary precursor of their later bilateral talks.

Bilateral talks: Heads of Agreement

By Thursday 15 October, Stephen had realized that the pseudo-plenary make-up of the Sub-Committee was preventing progress, and he announced the suspension of the Committee in favour of bilateral meetings with one party at a time. Immediately, a little of the fog began to clear. The bilateral arrangement precluded any point-scoring or abuse, and kept parties focused on the business in hand. Within a week, it led to a trilateral with the UUP and the Irish delegation on 22 October, another the following day, and a third the following week. The switch also coincided with adoption of Mayhew's (and Andrew's) plea for a broadening of the agenda across all three Strands and a reorientation of business towards the production of a Heads of Agreement.

Not only did this reduce the level of rhetoric and argument around the table, it also allowed Stephen to bring together particular parties to focus on particular issues, far away from the formal agenda. Thus it is that both Dublin and the Ulster Unionists began to see hints of progress over the North–South relationship, and indeed were soon heading towards defining the modalities of a deal which would swap change to the Articles in return for enhanced North–South executive power. It was a thorny topic, fraught with domestic risks for both sides, but one that they did make some progress on:

> We thought we had UUP agreement to an expression of the degree to which the North–South entity would have executive powers. And there was a fair bit of excitement on the part of the Irish as well. On the part of Flynn in particular, whom I remember at a late-night meeting saying, 'Yes! We're going to crack this!' and really getting quite excited. (Thompson)

But however realistic or otherwise such hopes of 'cracking it' might have been, unfortunately, the external bombshell of the Irish general election very effectively put paid to them. Nonetheless, the memories of serious dialogue and movement remained with those involved. The Australians made a substantial and lasting contribution to the long-term process. Many obstacles were indeed 'stockpiled', but only after having been examined and discussed in great detail: if they were not overcome, they were certainly far better understood by all concerned. That learning was of major assistance to future efforts, offering a smooth, authoritative, directed yet flexible framework within which the parties developed much greater accuracy of understanding of each other and their positions, and of the issues and obstacles before them. While ultimately nothing was agreed, ultimately nothing was forgotten either. In 1996, the learning from Stephen's facilitation meant that new talks did not start from scratch but rather built on that previous progress.

Appendix 1
The *Possible Outline Framework* Papers

10 June 1992

Sub-Committee Report

1   The sub-Committee met on 5 June and adjourned as a mark of respect to the victims of the accident near Carrickfergus the evening before.

2   It met again on 8, 9 and 10 June.

3   The sub-Committee continued, as mandated by plenary on foot of the 1 June report of the sub-Committee established on 26 May, to work towards the greatest possible degree of common ground on new political institutions for Northern Ireland. What plenary did on that occasion was to:

— 'authorise the sub-Committee, building on the Common Themes and Common Principles documents and the provisional report of the Structures sub-Committee (dated 13 May), to work towards the greatest possible degree of common ground on new political institutions for Northern Ireland, by addressing issues including those listed in paragraph 5 of that report, recognising that each party may wish to reserve its position on particular points;

— acknowledge that in order to secure a generally acceptable outcome from the Talks process it will be necessary to ensure that the outcome, taken as a whole, gives expression to the identities of both main parts of the Northern Ireland community and would attract the widest possible degree of allegiance and support; and

— further acknowledge that the course of discussions during Strands II and III may make it appropriate in the view of one party or another to propose that relevant matters in Strand I should be reviewed.'

4 It may be convenient to recall at this point that the sub-Committee which reported on 13 May had noted certain areas where, although there was broad agreement in principle (some reflected in the Common Themes paper), further detailed consideration would be necessary once the broad shape of the key institutional arrangements was clear. These include:

(a) 'an acknowledgement, consistent with paragraph 2 of the Common Themes paper, that the United Kingdom Government and Parliament would continue to have sovereign responsibility for all matters for which responsibility was not transferred to any new political institutions in Northern Ireland;

(b) an acknowledgement that the Secretary of State would continue to be wholly accountable to Parliament at Westminster for the exercise of any powers and responsibilities which he would retain, coupled with a general concern (expressed in particular by the UUP and DUP) to ensure appropriate parliamentary scrutiny of and accountability for the exercise by the Secretary of State of those powers and responsibilities;

(c) the need to make arrangements to secure a local political input to the exercise of those powers and responsibilities, especially in respect of security matters (if they continued to be the responsibility of HMG);

(d) the need to define a clear relationship between any new political institutions in Northern Ireland and EC institutions;

(e) what should be the precise nature and role of the Assembly and any Committees thereof, including in respect of legislation;

(f) a requirement for arrangements for determining expenditure levels in Northern Ireland, allocating resources and ensuring a strong role for the Assembly in the scrutiny of budgetary proposals, together with a consideration of the extent, if any, to which any new political institutions might have revenue-raising powers; and

(g) machinery to deal with the correct grievances and to entrench individual and community rights, including the possibility of a Bill of Rights.'

5   The sub-Committee sought to confirm and expand the areas of common ground identified in the Possible Outline Framework for new political institutions in Northern Ireland produced at 0045 on 3 June. It was able to expand in a number of minor respects the area of common ground it represented. A revised version is attached as Annex A. The UDUP, UUP and Alliance Party agreed that executive and legislative responsibilities in respect of transferred matters should be exercised through an elected Assembly, though they were prepared to contemplate a role for a separately-elected Panel in certain circumstances. The SDLP reserved its position on the source of the authority of Heads of Departments and their relationship with Departmental Committees; and on the arrangements for legislation in the transferred field.

6   The sub-Committee also agreed a paper (Annex B), subject to certain reservations, describing the elements of a Code of Practice setting out roles and responsibilities for Departments, Assembly Committees and the Assembly as a whole. In doing so it took account of two papers from the Government on the machinery of government in Northern Ireland and public appointments procedures. It also noted a paper from the Government Team (Annex C) on possible measures for ensuring an appropriate, fair and significant role for all main political traditions in Northern Ireland. Related papers on one aspect of this topic tabled by each of the four parties are at Annexes C1–C4.

7   The sub-Committee achieved a considerable measure of agreement in respect of the relationship between any new political institutions in Northern Ireland and the Westminster Parliament, and the UK Government system more generally; and the relationship with EC institutions. Reports on these subjects are at Annexes D and E.

8   The Parties represented on the sub-Committee also received, but did not collectively consider, discussion papers on finance, human rights, a Bill of Rights and cultural expression and diversity.

9   In submitting their report to plenary the members of the sub-Committee wish to express their thanks to Mr Hanley, Mr Chilcott and Mr Fell for their chairmanship of the

sub-Committee's deliberations, to the officials and other staff who supported the sub-Committee and to the delegates and the party delegations more widely for the hard work they put in.

Annex A
New Political Institutions in Northern Ireland
Possible Outline Framework (to assist discussion)

1 There would be a single, unicameral Assembly of 85 members elected by proportional representation and a separate election from a single Northern Ireland constituency to a panel of three people with significant consultative, monitoring, referral and representational functions.

2 The institutions would have executive and legislative responsibilities over at least as wide a range of subjects as in 1973 with scope for further transfers if the arrangements proved stable and durable and there was agreement on how to exercise such powers. Executive responsibilities would be discharged through Northern Ireland Government Departments, the Heads of which would be drawn from the Assembly.

3 The Secretary of State would remain accountable to Westminster for matters which were not transferred.

The Assembly

4 The Assembly would be presided over by a Speaker; election would be by a weighted majority, of say 70%, of the Assembly. The Assembly would exercise its powers through a system of Departmental Committees, with Chairmanships, Deputy Chairmanships and memberships allocated broadly in proportion to party strengths in the Assembly. The Chairmen of the Departmental Committees could be Heads of Departments. Non-departmental Committees would include a Business Committee and a General Purposes Committee with co-ordinating functions.

5 A 'code of practice' would specify the respective roles, responsibilities and decision taking powers of Departments, Assembly Committees and the Assembly at large.

6 Legislative procedures would be prescribed by constitutional legislation. All legislation could require the support of (at least)

a majority of both the relevant Committee and the full Assembly. Certain important legislation (e.g. a financial measure, one with constitutional implications, or significant implications for community relations), could require weighted majority approval (of say 70%). Other measures might be dealt with on the basis of majority decision unless, for example, the Business Committee determined they were contentious or a petition to that effect secured a certain threshold of say 30% support in the Assembly.

7 The constitutional legislation for establishing new institutions would provide for machinery to deal with and correct grievances and would provide for the further entrenchment of individual and community rights, including through a Bill of Rights, which the Assembly could not amend.

8 The allocation of chairmanships between Committees would be made in accordance with party strengths, perhaps in accordance with the D'Hondt Rule. Any acceptable option for allocation must however ensure that the system of government provides an appropriate, fair and significant role for representatives of all main traditions in Northern Ireland.

9 Committee Chairmanships would normally last for the whole term of the Assembly. Chairmen of the Departmental Committees might be included as members of the General Purposes Committee. Further consideration will be given to means to prevent Chairmen becoming captives of their Committees. Chairmen, whose appointment would be formally ratified by the Assembly, would be accountable to the Assembly, including through answering questions.

10 Departmental Estimates, policies and actions would be subject to scrutiny by the relevant Committee, which would have the power to compel attendance, call for papers etc. The Assembly would debate reports from, and the minutes of, each Committee.

11 Further consideration will be given to whether a mechanism is necessary to exclude from any share of executive power, or more generally, any individuals or representatives of parties who condone the use of violence for political ends.

The Panel

12 The panel might have a general duty, acting by consensus to consult, formally and informally, with the Assembly and with the Secretary of State and to give advice.

13 The panel's rights/powers and responsibilities (including statutory duties) and procedures would need to be carefully defined. For example, it could have powers in respect of proposed legislation, to determine (i.e. to accept, reject, give an opinion on or propose amendments to) and propose legislation referred to it under procedures to be agreed. It might, by consensus, refer any proposed legislation for some form of judicial consideration.

14 It could have a supportive role in the public expenditure cycle, liaising with the Secretary of State over the setting of total Northern Ireland public expenditure. It could also be an arbiter in settling public expenditure allocation disputes between Departments, having regard to the views of Heads of Departments and the Finance Committee.

15 The panel might have power, by consensus, to approve designated public appointments made in respect of transferred matters. It could also advise the Secretary of State in respect of any appointments within his responsibility.

16 It could also have powers in relation to administrative actions or proposed actions, perhaps on the basis of a referral by a threshold vote within the Assembly.

17 The panel could have a duty to prepare for the Assembly and for the Secretary of State regular (annual) reports on their own activities and their view of the operation of the new political institutions.

18 The panel could also have an important representational and promotional role. It could have a special commitment to the economic development of Northern Ireland, through participation in joint promotional activities in collaboration with the appropriate agencies.

19 The panel might secure its share of resources from the Secretary of State independently from the rest of the 'transferred' block in order to ensure both its financial independence, and that its resources were sufficient to carry out the work.

Annex B
'Code of Practice'

Introduction

1   The Possible Outline Framework for new political institutions in Northern Ireland (Annex A) says that a 'Code of Practice' would specify the respective roles, responsibilities and decision-taking powers of Departments, Assembly Committees and the Assembly at large. This paper draws on existing practice and precedent to suggest a possible specification.

2   It was proposed by the UDUP and agreed by the UUP and the Alliance Party that the paper should also suggest a possible basis for distinguishing the relative roles and responsibilities of Committee Chairmen and Committees in circumstances where executive responsibilities rested with Departmental Committees of the Assembly and/or their Chairmen. The SDLP reserved its position on the source of the authority of Heads of Departments and their relationship with the Departmental Committees; and on the arrangements for legislation in the transferred field.

Departments

3   Under any new political arrangements, each Department would have the following roles and responsibilities:

(a) to administer programmes fairly and efficiently;

(b) to administer programmes in a way conducive to promoting good community relations and equality of treatment;

(c) to implement agreed policy and to support the Head of the Department and/or the relevant Departmental Committee in seeking to develop and secure support for proposed policies;

(d) to advise the Head of the Department and/or the relevant Departmental Committee on proposed policy changes, on new initiatives or on the handling of particular issues with a degree of political significance;

(e) to liaise with other Departments on matters where there are overlapping interests so that co-ordinated or at least complementary advice can be put to the respective Heads of Departments and/or the relevant Departmental Committees;

(f) to maintain official-level contact with relevant organisations and interest groups within Northern Ireland and with relevant bodies elsewhere with a view to promoting the policy objectives set for the Department and ensuring that it is in a position to advise the Head of Department and/or the relevant Departmental Committee on developments, and to respond to those developments;

(g) to participate in the public expenditure survey cycle, led by DFP, and to advise the Head of Department and/or the relevant Departmental Committee ensuring the process of determining the Department's budget and in determining allocations between programmes;

(h) to have due regard to the requirements of public accountability;

(i) to keep its internal structures, management systems and resources under review to ensure they are adequate to meet requirements;

(j) to make certain public appointments and, in consultation with the Central Secretariat, to advise the Head of Department and/or the relevant Departmental Committee on other public appointments within the Department's sphere of responsibility;

(k) to assist the Head of the Department and/or the relevant Departmental Committee to respond to representations, whether from elected representatives or other interest groups;

(l) to advise the Head of Department and/or the relevant Departmental Committee on measures to promote awareness of and to attract public support for current or proposed policies.

Assembly Committees

4   A Business Committee would be established to co-ordinate Assembly business.

5   A General Purposes Committee, the members of which could include the Chairmen of Departmental Committees, would be established to assist in co-ordinating the interests of the relevant Committees in respect of issues which cross Departmental boundaries.

6   Other non-Departmental Committees might be established to act as a focus for the Assembly interest in particular areas, such as non-transferred matters, cultural expression and diversity and relationships with bodies or institutions outside Northern Ireland.

7   Annex B1 suggests a basis for distinguishing the relative roles

and responsibilities of Departmental Committee Chairmen and Committees. As noted in paragraph 2 above, the SDLP reserved its position on this point.

8 Departmental Committees might have the following roles and responsibilities:

(a) to participate in the arrangements for determining the Department's budgetary allocations, possible on the lines set out in Annex B2;

(b) to scrutinise the work of the relevant Department and non-Departmental public bodies;

(c) to hold hearings, whether public or private, for which purpose it would have powers to compel the attendance of relevant persons and call for papers;

(d) to prepare reports, with recommendations including proposals for legislation, on major policy issues. These might involve liaison with other Departmental Committees, including the Finance Committee

(e) to consider legislation in the transferred field, including considering proposals for new legislation and taking at least the Committee stage of relevant primary legislation unless the Assembly, on the recommendation of the Business Committee or the General Purpose Committee, decides otherwise. Committees might also debate secondary legislation;

(f) to act as a forum for the expression of local political views on the area of responsibility of the relevant Department.

9 In drawing up reports, making recommendations and debating legislation Departmental Committees would operate on the basis of majority decision-making in respect of routine non-contentious matters. There could, however, be provision for weighted voting in certain circumstances especially in respect of contentious matters; or for dissenting reports; or for a significant minority on any Committee to have power to defer the consideration of proposed legislation or administrative actions or to refer such issues for consideration by the Assembly at large.

The Assembly at large

10 The Assembly at large might be expected to have at least the following main roles and responsibilities:

(a) to elect a Speaker (by a weighted majority vote of say 70%);

(b) to appoint the Chairmen, Deputy Chairmen and members of Departmental and other Committees. The Chairmanships and Deputy Chairmanships (at least) of the Departmental Committees might be allocated by a formula, perhaps the D'Hondt procedure calculated on the basis of political party strengths in the Assembly following the elections. Other arrangements might be made to determine the allocation of individual members of Committees though each party should have a share of the total Committee places broadly proportional to its strength in the Assembly;

(c) to hold Heads of Departments and/or the relevant Departmental Committee accountable for the work of their Department through

— Questions
— adjournment debates
— debates on Statements
— emergency debates
— consideration of reports from Departments
— consideration of minutes and reports from Departmental Committees
— consideration of reports from
  • Comptroller and Auditor General
  • Examiner of Statutory Rules?
  • Ombudsman
  • FEC [Fair Employment Commission]
  • EOC [Equal Opportunities Commission]
  • other statutory bodies

(possibly on the basis of further reports from the relevant Committee);

(d) (subject to the SDLP's reservation on arrangements for legislation in the transferred field) to legislate in the transferred field (and in the excepted or reserved field where ancillary to Westminster legislation or with the consent of the Secretary of State). The precise distribution of the legislative process as between Committees and the full Assembly may require further consideration. Different arrangements might apply in respect of primary and secondary legislation (whether subject to affirmative resolution or negative resolution).

11 Legislation would require the support of at least a majority of

the full Assembly. Certain important legislation (e.g. a financial measure, one with constitutional implications or significant implications for community relations) could require weighted majority approval, of say 70%. Other legislation could require weighted majority approval if it was deemed to be contentious by the Business Committee or a petition to that effect secured a certain threshold of say 30% support in the Assembly;

(e) where requested, to make recommendations to the Secretary of State on certain legislation in the reserved field to be made at Westminster;

(f) to consider minutes and reports from the Business Committee and any other non-Departmental Committees which might be established;

(g) to refer certain issues (on the basis of a threshold level of say 30% support in the Assembly) for consideration by the Panel. Those issues might include proposed legislation and administrative actions;

(h) to act as a forum for the expression of political views within Northern Ireland.

Annex B1
The Relative Roles and Responsibilities of Committee Chairmen and Committees

1 In circumstances where executive responsibilities rested with Departmental Committees of the Assembly the efficient conduct of business and the need to ensure an appropriate, fair and significant role for all main traditions in Northern Ireland would require clear guidance to be drawn up on the respective roles of Committee Chairmen and the Committees as a whole.

2 Administratively, it would be appropriate for Chairmen alone (and perhaps Deputy Chairmen in certain circumstances) to have full access to Departmental officials and papers in the same way as Ministers do at present. it could also be appropriate for the Committee as a whole to be serviced by Assembly staff, rather than Departmental staff. The Committee's power to call for persons and papers would enable it to have access to Departmental officials and papers but conventions would need to be established to preserve the distinct role of the Chairmen

and protect certain information which requires to be kept confidential (e.g. relating to inward investment decisions).

3   The Committee would have a significant role in determining policy directions, e.g. through being required to authorise the Departmental Estimates going before the Assembly, to approve the Department's bid to the Business Committee for a legislative programme for the year and to approve capital expenditure decisions above a certain level. It could also establish broad lines of policy in particular areas on foot of reports it might make following detailed consideration of a particular issue.

4   The Chairman, supported by the Department, could be expected to have a major influence on all such decisions but would then be expected to act in conformity with them.

5   At the level of day-to-day administration, decisions could be categorised in a number of ways. One possibility would be to distinguish:

(a) those which Departments would make on their own initiative;

(b) those which in the judgement of the Committee Chairman would not require prior Committee approval and which the Committee Chairman would make on his or her own initiative, within the general policy framework established by the Committee (see paragraph 3). All or some of these would be notified to the Committee as a whole, giving the Committee an opportunity to indicate its satisfaction or otherwise and to determine whether similar decisions should in future be handled in a different way or brought to the Committee for consideration;

(c) those which in the judgement of the Committee Chairman would require the prior approval of the Committee as a whole. Some guidance would be drawn up in advance to illustrate which types of decision would be likely to fall into this category. The circumstances of the individual Northern Ireland Departments vary and it is unlikely that a standard formula could apply equally to all; but the types of decision which would be politically sensitive or crucial to the Department in policy terms, are likely to be reasonably clear in each case.

Footnote:

Arrangements on these lines could result in a committee Chairman being held accountable (see paragraph 10(c) of Annex B) in the

Assembly for policies which he or she did not personally support. In those circumstances arrangements analogous to those which apply when an Accounting Officer is overruled by his or her political Head might come into play and enable the Chairman to discharge the accountability requirement by pointing to a formal record of his or her views being overridden by the Committee.

Annex B2
Departmental Budgetary Allocation Process

1   This note sets out arrangements for determining Departments' budgetary allocations in the circumstances where executive responsibilities rested with Departmental Committees of the Assembly. The SDLP reserved its position on these arrangements.

2   Each Department would build up its bid for resources through participation in the normal Public Expenditure Survey mechanisms. The relevant Departmental Committee would be invited to endorse the Department's bid before it was finalised. The Finance Committee would then consider all the bids and seek to produce an agreed allocation between Departments of the available resources. If it failed the matter might be referred to the Panel for arbitration.

3   Once each Department's allocation was settled the Chairman would propose Departmental Estimates for the coming year to the Committee and seek its approval, line by line, to the detailed distribution of that allocation to individual Departmental programmes.

4   The approved Departmental Estimates would then be put formally to the full Assembly whose role would be to authorise expenditure on the basis of those Estimates.

Footnote:

This is very much a broad outline of how the arrangements might work. The Public Expenditure Survey procedures are complex and iterative and many detailed adjustments would need to be made to bring them fully into line with the principles set out above.

Appendix 2

The 'Ninian Stephen Document', 26 October 1992

This document was sent to Sinn Fein by the British Government

[Extract from Sinn Fein: *Setting the Record Straight*, Belfast 1993, pp. 19–20

A note on the provenance of this document:
In 1993, after considerable denial by Mayhew and by Major (who had claimed publicly that 'talking to terrorists would turn my stomach'), the existence of the secret British–Sinn Fein communication channel was leaked by an NIO official to the DUP. Mayhew's response was a rather fancifully edited and very partisan version of the dialogue. In reply, Sinn Fein published a far more complete version of the exchanges in 'Setting the Record Straight' in order to demonstrate the depth and substance of the dialogue. Although no absolute certainty can be claimed, the Sinn Fein version proved in many ways to be far more accurate than the British one, which contained many factual errors and omissions.]

1   Intensive shuttle diplomacy on the part of Sir N Stephen. Atmosphere improves.

2   On 16 [14] October SOSNI [Secretary of State for Northern Ireland] had a short meeting with the Irish. Both Governments agreed that the best chance of progress lay in the proposal that Sir Ninian Stephen should invite all the talks participants to submit to him privately their individual suggestions for Heads of Agreement across all three Strands. It was a high risk strategy, but Sir Ninian appeared well aware of the extreme delicacy of the task and the importance of getting his synthesis right first time. There was a slight danger that Sir Ninian's report would be based on the lowest common denominator of the parties' submissions and thus not form the basis of a workable blueprint; this was a risk which would have to be taken.

3   On the afternoon of 16 [14] October there was a short session of the Strand 2 committee. Sir Ninian formally asked the parties to submit to him, either orally or in writing, their ideas for Heads of Agreement, their concept of the areas where their proposals agreed with those of other delegations, and their views on any areas where they perceived disagreements to exist. Sir Ninian would then correlate the submissions with his own impressions and formulate his report. He had no preconceptions about the form the report would take, and indeed he realised that there was disagreement between the participants as to the scope of the exercise; he saw the process as being a dynamic one which would assume a more coherent form during the course of the following week's consultations.

4   On timetable, Sir Ninian suggested that 19 and 20 October be taken up with bilateral consultations with the NI political parties and that he should talk to the two Governments separately on 21 and 22 October. On 23 October he would report progress to the entire sub-committee either orally or on paper. This, however, he stressed, was only an outline, and changes could be made if people felt it desirable. In addition, he encouraged the delegations to talk to each other as much as possible.

5   These proposals were accepted, albeit with some reservation by the SDLP.

6   The talks have thus entered an entirely new stage. Sir Ninian is now effectively in control of all three Strands and the nature of his proposed shuttle diplomacy over the next week (and possibly for longer) means that events could begin to develop very quickly. Information about who is saying what to whom will be at a premium.

7   In preparation for its meeting with Sir Ninian on 21 October the HMG [Her Majesty's Government] team is drawing up a model Heads of Agreement which it believes stand the widest chance of being accepted by all concerned. These will be submitted for his use on as non-attributable basis, in an attempt to guide his consultations. The idea is to 'ghost-write' Sir Ninian's report. The main elements are as follows:

  • Strand 1. Based closely on the Strand 1 sub-committee report of earlier in the year [10 June], with the chairmen of Assembly committees becoming heads of department, and with the Assembly being the sole legislative authority but having to submit draft legislation to the separate 'Panel' for ratification.

- Strand 2. This envisages co-operation between respective departments in the North and the South, the establishment of cross-border executive agencies by the respective legislatures North and South and remaining answerable to them, and the delivery of some all-Ireland executive functions by the body itself, subject to democratic approval and accountability.

- Strand 3. An IGC [Inter-Governmental Conference] and Secretariat to deal with non-transferred matters affecting NI, with Panel members and committee chairmen from NI formally part of the IGC structure. On the constitutional status of the Province, a statement that NI is currently part of the UK is proposed together with a recognition that a substantial minority wish for a united Ireland, and have the right to pursue that by peaceful and democratic means and without impediment. Replacement of Articles 2 and 3 of the Irish Constitution by an aspiration to a united Ireland is also sought.

  The paper, it is stressed, represents HMG's judgement of what it is possible to achieve, rather than its own sense of priorities in individual areas.

8   If an outline agreement something along these lines is possible there may be a chance of the parties reconvening to put flesh on the bones at some point in the future after the 16 November IGC. Events in the next couple of weeks could move rapidly and unpredictably.

Note: Reports up to this point on the Stormont talks had been pessimistic in outlook. When the unfounded optimism contained in the 'Ninian Stephen' document subsided, Sinn Fein was informed that, given lack of progress in the Stormont talks, that [sic] the British and Irish governments were considering imposing a situation over the heads of the political parties.

Bibliography

Bloomfield, David, 1997. *Peacemaking Strategies in Northern Ireland: building complementarity in conflict management theory*. London, Macmillan.

Bloomfield, David, 1998. *Political Dialogue in Northern Ireland: the Brooke Initiative, 1989–92*. London, Macmillan.

Prior, Jim, 1986. *A Balance of Power*. London, Hamish Hamilton.

Sinn Fein, 1993. *Setting the Record Straight: a record of communications between Sinn Fein and the British government, October 1990 – November 1993*. Belfast, Sinn Fein.

Index